P9-AET-709

The Root of the Thing

A Study of Job and
The Song of Songs

Other Books by Albert Cook

The Dark Voyage and the Golden Mean
The Meaning of Fiction
Oedipus Rex: *A Mirror for Greek Drama*
Progressions and Other Poems
The Odyssey (verse translation)
The Classic Line: *A Study in Epic Poetry*
Prisms: *Studies in Modern Literature*
The Charges: *Poems*

223.1
C771

the Root of the Thing

A Study of Job and The Song of Songs

WITHDRAWN

ALBERT COOK

97749

1968
Indiana University Press
Bloomington and London

LIBRARY ST. MARY'S COLLEGE

Copyright © 1968 by Albert Cook

All rights reserved

No part of this book may be reproduced or utilized in any form or by any means, electronic or mechanical, including photocopying and recording, or by any information storage and retrieval system, without permission in writing from the publisher. The Association of American University Presses' Resolution on Permissions constitutes the only exception to this prohibition.

Published in Canada by Fitzhenry & Whiteside Limited, Scarborough, Ontario

Library of Congress catalog card number: 68-27340

Manufactured in the United States of America

To Francis Williams and
John Pairman Brown,
Brothers in the Way

Contents

Acknowledgments

I should like to thank the Research Foundation of the State University of New York for a summer grant on which I began this book, and the Center for Advanced Study in the Behavioral Sciences for the fellowship on which I completed it in substantially its present form. John Pairman Brown, Laurence Michel and Francis Williams have helped me by making suggestions towards improvement, and my research assistants Mark Riley, Thomas A. Duddy, and Phillip Bodrock have sought out and verified references. I am grateful as well to Bernard Perry and Dorothy Wikelund of the Indiana University Press for bearing with the manuscript through various stages, and for sensitive editorial assistance. My deepest debt is to my wife, for the spirit that makes all possible.

A Note on the Text

The superb poetry of the King James Version recommends it for citation, as its moderate fidelity to the Hebrew original legitimizes its use. An alternative might have been to produce my own version, but my incapacities, and either indolence or economy, have kept me from doing that. My limits have therefore freed me from any temptation to slant a rendering, as later translators so often do, in order to reinforce some particular interpretation. In order to interpret at all, of course, especially in Job, I have been forced to choose among alternate readings. And where I follow good opinion in faulting the King James Version, I have simply indicated its probable errors.

Readers unfamiliar with the King James Version should especially notice its helpful practice of italicizing in the English all words for which no corresponding word exists in the Hebrew.

Ich spüre übrigens immer wieder, wie alttestamentlich ich denke und empfinde; so habe ich in den vergangenen Monaten auch viel mehr Altes Testament als Neues Testament gelesen. Nur wenn man die Unaussprechlichkeit des Namens Gottes kennt, darf man auch einmal den Namen Jesus Christus aussprechen; nur wenn man das Leben und die Erde so liebt, dass mit ihr alles verloren und zu Ende zu sein scheint, darf man an die Auferstehung der Toten und eine neue Welt glauben; nur wenn man das Gesetz Gottes über sich gelten lässt, darf man wohl auch einmal von Gnade sprechen, und nur wenn der Zorn und die Rache Gottes über seine Feinde als gültige Wirklichkeiten stehen bleiben, kann von Vergebung und von Feindesliebe etwas unser Herz berühren. Wer zu schnell und zu direkt neutestamentlich sein und empfinden will, ist m. E. kein Christ. Wir haben darüber ja schon manchmal gesprochen und jeder Tag bestätigt mir, dass es richtig ist. Man kann und darf das letzte Wort nicht vor dem vorletzten sprechen. Wir leben im Vorletzten und glauben das Letzte, ist es nicht so?

—Dietrich Bonhoeffer, *Auswahl*, Munich, 1964, p. 547

Preface

Job and The Song of Songs, from the same section, "Writings," of the Bible's ancient tripartite division, speak with special emphasis to the modern spirit.

Job, through its confrontation of a radical perplexity in human existence, forcefully sets "the problem of evil" and "the problem of pain" into a form that has evoked prolonged, mature comment from thinkers as different as Josiah Royce and Carl Jung. And The Song of Songs serves easily as a hymn praising not only the direct erotic fulfillment of lovers but the full primacy and power of Eros as it can be felt in every sphere, and at every depth, of our lives.

As it happens, these books do have a special character, as well as a special interest, that differentiates them from the rest of the Bible: they are cast in dramatic form. They also have a special relationship to the rest of the Old Testament, and to the New. The canonicity of The Song of Songs was long in doubt, and Job was repeatedly shifted from one position to another in the "Writings." Moreover, the Song strangely uses the divine name only once (and then not certainly) in a Scripture that elsewhere abounds in repetitions of the terms for God. Job, on the other hand, presents an unparalleled variety of such terms.

The isolation of these books in the canon may be measured by the echoes and citations from them in the New Testament, which assumed its present shape not too long after the canon of the Old had been established. While there are 276 references to Isaiah in the New Testament and 279 to Psalms, there are only ten to Job, and to the Song none whatever. Of the ones to Job, many are questionable and vague; for instance, 1 Thessalonians 5:22, "Abstain from all appearance of evil," is supposed to echo Job 1:1, "that man . . . eschewed evil." But even if all ten are accepted, Job would not bulk large in the New Testament authors' sense of their Old Testament canon.

For all this special character, Job and The Song of Songs do belong to the canon, and this general fact has literary consequences, as does their dramatic form. What are the implications of "Bible"? Of "drama"?

The Root of the Thing

A Study of Job and
The Song of Songs

1 Bible Drama

BIBLE

"Literature" does not have always, and primarily, just the function of expanding the mind and feelings of private men, as it has been conceived since the Renaissance. Into a literary statement is built, as part of its statement, the full expectation of what a member of the given group intends when he makes one. In a burst of chant, the workman intends the word to aid a monotonous act towards being charmed by its own monotony: the word lulls. The Chinese official in the province indites a verse to perk up a few friends by whiling away time, when they too have to while away time; in the recognition they will grow closer. The minnesinger charms a court, the rhapsode a tribe.

"The Bible equals the revealed Word of God." We do not, at this present, very altered time, have to assent to this proposition, for the conception of Inspiration to inhere in the Book. Ancient Israel, when it receives utterances into its national literature and classifies them as authentic, thereby defines its national literature as a Bible; and identifies literature with scripture. That identification, as it is confirmed and reintegrated into a present Church in some ways discontinuous from the history of that Israel, may be reaffirmed under the acceptance of ecclesiastical authority. (It might be denied to a *Koran*, and still the book would possess the *literary* character of a scripture.) In any case, the scriptural is the first of the uses of the initial identification that canonizes the books in our Bible together.

There are several other uses, the most familiar of which to us is, again, the Renaissance one, of private identification, a use given the special name of Reformation when the book entering the new, private domain of expanding consciousness is taken to be the Book of maximum authority.

The assertion contained within the shape of Biblical utterance, that the word is a Word, begins in our time to draw close to the romantic assertion that any words properly inspired create a Word. And so, in the theology of inspiration, the religious notion that words are prayers no matter what, may draw close to the secular notion that words are instruments no matter what. The instrument is a prayer, the prayer an instrument, in the secular city; and this would hold for special uses as well as for general: it would even hold for readers in the more restrictedly "literary" culture which those Calvinists-of-the-sensibility, Arnold and Babbitt, wished to erect into a special religious instrument of moral definition, every man his own intuitive canon lawyer and casuist. Even their finely tooled instrumentality may be construed as a prayer—and so also may be the general instrumentality of saying a loving word to another person, a possibility open to all who speak the same language, while Arnold's "culture" is open only to the privileged at any time.

The loving attention we are able to direct toward turning the instrument into a prayer may converge upon a Word whose instruments, the constituent words, are framed to constitute something religious for which "prayer" will do as well as another word. (Other traditional terms are "witness," "testament," and "law," *torah*.) The Bible, then, eases this particular act of loving attention to literature by declaring implicitly that it constitutes a prayer (or witness or law or prophecy or wisdom). It is already what our attention would will it to be. To call the Bible "literature" would then be either a tautology, if we wish to mean by literature what it implicitly declares itself to be; or else it would be an error, where we violate history by wrenching it to the particular post-Renaissance uses of literature and read Isaiah as framing his verses from the same deep motive as Keats, or Job as though its author used a form only accidentally different from that of the author of *King Lear*.

The historical complex of its utterances is set into a total literary statement as integrally as a historical complex is set into the individual constituents of the statement, its words. Those changing sense-packets are fixed beyond change at the codified moment of being written down. The words tell of their temporal origins as well as serve the order of the work where they occur. All poems are pretty, or we could not call them poems. Yet the Chinese official means something different from the chanting workman, as the minnesinger does from the rhapsode; and all differ from the self-declared poet balancing his other acts by that monumental self-declaration in the modern city.

Our institutions for attention to literature, our universities, respond intensely, with love or in some cases hatred, to the intense declaration of the modern poet. For his verse and for the Bible equally, they would reassure themselves by subsuming literature under the categories it can take for granted. So they would present the Bible as something just pretty, on the untenable assumption that it can be (mis)"read" as "literature." Thus they wish to preserve the Keats-like elements actually present in scripture within a special alien social frame, consigning the law-like aspects of its fullness to another institution, the Church—which may itself be tempted to see the Bible as merely a verbal jigsaw puzzle of doctrinal apologetics.

Loving attention to the text in no way prejudices the extrapolations of apologetic theology, nor does it obtrude on the exact philological concerns of the editor. Lower criticism, higher criticism, and then the criticism known as literary, all converge on the text, as do the collective readings in a worship service, the constructive readings of apologists, and the devotional readings of the devout. We end as we begin, with the Book, whose circularity for us is a circularity it has declared in the historical set of its utterances over the reaches of its own time (and so ours). It directs its varieties of utterance toward a unified Book, and it holds them together between one set of covers for us, one scroll in the ark at its time, on whose "law" other scrolls comment with a declared maximum authority.

The word of the Hebrew text weights itself with signification. The selfsame word, *davar,* from a root that means "to speak" (also originally "to drive off," "to lead," "to follow," and " to consider"), covers the sense "word," and the sense "thing." *Davar* covers the Latin *verbum,* and also the Latin *res.* When Job says "the root of the matter is found in me," he uses *davar,* and we may render it as "the root of the thing," and also "the root of the word." Word and thing carry their identity in a conception of "literature" which draws all permanent statements into the sphere of the holy, situating the Word physically within the Holy of Holies on the high altar.

The Word as a whole receives that name only in Christian usage. Among the Israelites the core of it, the Pentateuch or Hexateuch, is known as the Law, the *torah,* and that law is conceived of as identical with the law of instruction (*torah* from *yarah,* "to instruct") conveyed orally by the priest:

> For the law shall not perish from the priest,
> Nor counsel from the wise, nor the word from the prophet
> (Jer. 18.18)

("Law" is *torah,* "word" is *davar.*) One can see, under this threefold division, a more or less explicit echo of the three traditional Hebrew divisions of scripture into Law, Prophecy, and Writings. One of these deals mainly with the past or eternal, the Law; the second deals with the future or eternal, Prophecy; and the last, a part of it sometimes called Wisdom, deals indifferently with present, past, and future, and also with the eternal. All are scripture; permanent writings are drawn into the sphere of the holy just as the secular actions of the chosen people are sacralized. We may find in the separate books of scripture a rough historical sequence: Law comes roughly before Prophecy and Prophecy before Wisdom. But that linear sequence takes on a secondary character before the primary act of canonizing the books together into a scripture, perhaps in connection with finding the Law in the Temple in 621 B.C. If that date is taken, then the circle is left open for some other books (including both Job and the Song, written after that date).

The nature of this canonization, possibly revolutionary but certainly also gradual, both complicates diachronically and simplifies synchronically the observations we are able to make about this literary tradition, in comparison with most others. For in them the primary sequence is one from an early poetry to a later prose standing beside other poetry.

In just this respect, the Bible offers verse in the midst of prose, each affecting the functions of the other. Jacob blesses his sons in verse at the end of Genesis, a prose account of remote origins. Deborah exults over a signal victory in verse, as Moses exults over a signal transit in verse, out of the context of sober but equally "holy" prose narrative.

In the prophets, verse takes over for whole books, but prose never drops away wholly as a possibility, and Jeremiah and Ezekiel use it freely where Amos had not. The oracular utterances of the Preacher in Ecclesiastes, framed first in prose, rise to a crescendo of verse at the end of the book. Job frames its verse dialogue with a prose narrative. The prose comments profoundly on the verse, and the other way around.

DRAMA

Here in the Bible, and here alone but for The Song of Songs, there occurs still another verbal structure, that of drama. There is no evidence for thinking that the drama in the Bible was ever performed, though The Song of Songs carries reminiscences of a drama-like marriage ritual. All the more abstractly, then, do the inherent features of a dramatic statement stand out as constituents of the "literary" statement in Bible drama, along with the more defined uses and interactions of poetry and prose.

The stage-group/audience framework, which underlies a formal dramatic statement, may be seen in the Bible, not only in Job and The Song of Songs but also in the prophets since they stand as speakers to an implied audience. Moreover, the prophets act out as well as speak their messages, describing the dramatization thereafter. Hosea does marry a prostitute, Jeremiah buy a piece of land, Isaiah name his sons, Ezekiel eat the book-wafer. They enact their message. Here, of course, as elsewhere in the deep urgency of the Bible, no stage illusion enters to keep the signs separated from what they designate. Instead the prophet founds the authenticity of what he designates on the actual enactment of his signs.

His comment does translate the reality into an enactment. In his sacrificial self-dramatization the prophet intensifies his comment by raising it to a level where word comes in afterwards to complete action, just as action had been produced to authenticate word. Instead of an imagined stage for words, the prophet offers an actuality in two different areas commenting on and supplementing each other.

Psalms, too, as a collective hymn-book, fuses the stage group with an audience group, because the speaker-group address themselves as well as God. Moreover, the identification of the single worshipper with the group becomes emphatic through the frequent use of the first person singular in grammatical form for a meaning that is, in effect, through group recitation, the first person plural. Thereby the stage-group and the audience also are identified. In Psalms the four (speaker, auditor, stage-group, audience) conflate, but the grammatical shifts, and the context of utterance, do make them distinguishable, elevating Psalms to a unified complexity beyond that of more ordinary hymns.

Job incorporates still more explicitly the form of dramatic dialogue. The great central section of the book occurs in dialogue, holding itself to the phenomenological point of verbal interchange. And something of the suppositiousness in a staged action is conveyed by the frame story: God is dramatizing for Satan Job's fidelity. The air of legendary reversion to the patriarchal past also makes the dialogue a re-creation for the reader.

Moreover, to some degree more than in Psalms, and even than in the writings of the prophets, the physical situation of the speakers in Job, the context of their location, carries significance: we are given something approaching a scene, one in which their withdrawal from the city allows the friends to speak undisturbed. The dung heap at Job's feet stages his despair, and the open universe surrounding all the speakers stages the cosmos, which keeps entering the dialogue, finally to dominate it.

The ritual silence of seven days which precedes the speeches constitutes a staged contrast, and analogy, to the speeches. As speeches they contrast with the silence: as occurring in the same ritual context they are an analogy to the silence, and borrow a devotedness from the ritual that they also, by contrast, are commenting upon.

God is a silent Spectator, along with us, and Elihu is a presumed silent spectator because his interruption is motivated by what he hears. He crosses the line, as we cannot, from audience to stage-group.

In Job and The Song of Songs, the scene is of course an imaginary one; nothing in the language sets an actual stage. At the same time, the imaginary scene is firmly designated by the dialogue. The fact that dialogue is the form, serves to widen the scene, as well as to draw a presumptive line between it and the implied audience. In The Song of Songs, we can almost surely not identify the audience wholly, even if we can partially, with the "daughters of Jerusalem" (Song, 1.5, 3.5, 5.8, 5.16, 8.4).

But dramatic speech heightens each speaker's expressiveness in these two books by building his utterances into the interactions of an imagined role in an imagined scene. The form of drama also intensifies the statements by complicating them. Any drama, to begin with, offers four possible sets of signifier-signified relationships: that (1) between the imagined scene and some actual scene; that (2) between the imagined group and their imagined scene; that (3) between the imagined group and the "audience" group; and finally that (4) between the audience group and their own actual scene. The complexities of the first three find their pay-off in the last, if the drama is handled well. If the drama is also scripture, the pay-off announces itself as of ultimate significance. As scripture, and as drama, Job and The Song of Songs manage their complexities so as to present the absorbing questions they may also be taken to answer.

II JOB
The Root of the Thing Is Found in Me

FRAME

In the context of the Bible, prose serves to narrate, plainly and succinctly, the events of sacred history, actual or suppositious. So it does even when it is used for prophetic purpose, and the prose of Ezekiel and Jeremiah, as it announces the visions of the prophets, echoes the straightforward accounts of Exodus and Samuel. Prose in the Writings may emphasize the suppositious or exemplary character of the narrative, as in Jonah, Ruth, and Esther where the tale of Mordecai, Marvin Pope comments,[1] begins with a formula emphasizing the discreteness of the narrative (as Job does) and Nathan's parable. Even the prose of Ecclesiastes, in echoing the tone of the rest of the canon, carries an association with narrative: the Preacher tells of his own state of mind, and the form of prose creates an expectation of story that the course of the book fulfills.

Job begins and ends as prose. As always in Biblical prose, the form of the language suggests narration, above and beyond the fact that indeed the book does begin as a straight narrative, "There was a man. . . ." The man was an actual patriarch, mentioned by Ezekiel (14.14, 20) along with Noah and Daniel, as a man who is also exemplary by virtue of his righteousness. Moreover, the man Job is remote enough in time (as much as a thousand years before the writing of the book), and in space (Uz is distant from Israel), to have about him an air of suppositiousness. The frame story sets up for him a suppositious and exemplary situation that demonstrates an integrity the concluding prose, again, draws back into the sphere of narrative actualization, prologue and epilogue being linked by specific echoes, as well as by the form of prose.

In the context of the Near East, again, the figure of the just man struck by misfortune appears often enough to make Job's situation a standard exemplum. The parallels to Job in Egyptian, Sumerian, and Babylonian literature may touch on other points of similarity, phrases, or even situations that recall Job's conversations with his friends or with God.

But the situation in Job deepens beyond standard exempla. Under the pressure of his misfortunes, Job has already uttered one verse more summary than any to be found in other Near Eastern texts. This verse is completely circular in its parallelism, and also completely circular in the affirmation it makes about his life:

> Naked came I out of my mother's womb,
> And naked shall I return thither:
> The Lord gave, and the Lord hath taken away;
> Blessed be the name of the Lord. (1.21)

Under the further pressure of suffering in his own body, the ritual of mourning for seven days with his silent friends does not suffice: that standard form does not meet the tremendous demands of a situation he senses far within himself to transcend even such utterances of total acceptance.

He begins the long questions of confrontation in the dramatic verse that occupies the bulk of the book and carries the fullest form of its affirmations. Now Job breaks wholly into verse, and verse serves as the swirling vehicle of tense affirmation, till God, having spoken in verse out of the whirlwind, relieves the pressure and slackens the tension by demanding of the friends a ritual sacrifice over Job.

The formal key signature of the narrative prose still remains through the book, in the tag phrases that announce the speakers. Verse heightens the speeches into another key signature, that of oracular summation and emotional outpouring. The tags provide the formal link, as do certain expressions common to both, between the prose part and the verse part. Moreover, the order of the parallelism in the verse speeches is dominant enough to influence parallel-like repetition in both prologue and epilogue. Prose begins and ends, verse dominates. Their interaction is never an interpenetration, and the set of each differs not only in the conventional range of its linguistic uses but also in the particular circumstance it surrounds. In the prose tale, God disproves Satan's allegation that Job's piety depends on his prosperity. In the verse drama, Job raises the question of why he must suffer, getting the answer, on a different plane, that God is inscrutably majestic. As the prose tale frames the verse drama, God is something like a stage manager who withholds the essential information that he is testing Job. But to take this as a straight dramatic irony would result in undercutting the force of God's statements from the whirlwind. That overriding voice would then be a Metternich-like device for concealing the true facts. Nor can one get from the suppositious test in the prose tale to the magnificent assertions of majesty at the climax of the verse drama: their interaction is not one of logical congruence. The prose frames, the verse transposes the terms ("integrity," "uprightness," "bless"); and verse occurs in an altered formal situation, since it takes up questions that transcend the suppositious situation of the tale.

Job suffers in the prose tale, seen from without. Seen from within, he must speak, and speak more than his initial verse of acceptance or prose of rebuke to his wife, "After this opened Job his mouth, and cursed his day" (3.1).

When Job breaks into a long speech, he breaks into extensive verse. Verse, strung tight and doubled back in the parallelism of its form, conveys the drama and signifies its outset.

But the action of drama, even such ritual-like action as lies behind the speeches of The Song of Songs, is absent from Job. The ritual actions, and all that has been acted upon Job before them, precede all the speeches.

The speeches of others do not so much act upon Job as arouse him to further speeches. Moreover, there is a clear base of common assumption which renders any stretch of a given speech nearly anonymous. The relative stasis of action in the verbal interchange has the effect of purifying the responsive flow of utterance. The more, then, do the responses enact a fusion of thought and emotion. To be sure, both are fused already in the Hebrew word *lev, levav,* which is usually translated "heart" but means "mind" as well.

All the speeches are in response to his own, and they center upon what he says. And since we know him from what he says, the interactions between the prose tale and the verse drama compose around the central figure "The root of the thing is found in me" (19.28b).[2]

INTEGRITY

Of common concern to both prose tale and verse drama in their juxtaposed unity, and central to the man at the center of both, is the integrity of Job, his wholeness. This quality is attributed to him at the very beginning; it is coupled with his uprightness in the first verse of the book. "And that man was perfect and upright, and one that feared God, and eschewed evil." God twice repeats this phrase (1.8, 2.3) in speaking to Satan. The word for "perfect," *tam,* refers to integrity, to the unblemished wholeness that makes a sacrificial animal fit to be offered to God. The unimpaired completeness it implies is taken for granted as an initial attribute of Job, one to be tested through the course of the book. Job "displays in a vivid and unforgettable form what it is to be a man of integrity."[3]

Through this integrity Job sustains both the outward test of the tale and the inward trial of the drama. He retains his wholeness. It is this wholeness, this integrity (*thummah*), that his wife urges him to abandon under suffering. "Dost thou still retain thine integrity? Curse God and die." (2.9)

His answer to her fulfills the condition that Satan has said he could not meet, "shall we receive good at the hand of God, and shall we not receive evil?" (2.10). But the full test of his integrity transcends even this initial condition. Once he has suffered in his body, once he has mourned and stood fast for seven days, he must still plumb the incongruity in his deep inward sense both of that integrity and of the justice of God. At one point he uses the word *tam* three times in the space of two verses:

> *If I say* I *am* perfect, it shall also prove me perverse.
> *Though* I *were* perfect, *yet* would I not know my soul:
> I would despise my life.
> This *is* one *thing*, therefore I said *it*,
> He destroyeth the perfect and the wicked. (9.20-22)

Here "perfect" remains the steadfast term[4] in three alternate propositions, (1) he would be proved perverse, (2) he would be proved ignorant, (3) God destroys the perfect and the wicked indifferently. All these, and especially the last, answer Bildad directly and pick up the term *tam* from him:

> Behold, God will not cast away a perfect man (8.20),

(though this is what God has seemed to do).

Eliphaz, like Job's wife, has used the word (*tom*, a variant of *thummah*, here rendered "uprightness") in his first speech to Job, in an initial clarity about the enigma posed by the integrity of his friend:

> *Is* not *this* thy fear, thy confidence,
> Thy hope, and the uprightness of thy ways? (4.6)

Through all the vacillations in his position and theirs, Job sustains the term (again rendered "upright"), though he comes to assert at some points a proposition even more severe than the third one above: God, far from being indifferent, singles the "just, upright" man out for mockery, "The just upright *man is* laughed to scorn." (12.4)

Eliphaz later implicitly continues to admit Job's integrity by reversing the question to ask what good God derives from a human perfection, "Or *is it* gain *to him,* that thou makest thy ways perfect?" (22.3) In the throes of his own continuing assertions, Job simply asserts that he will not let this essential quality go, "Till I die I will not remove mine integrity from me" (27.5). And he begins his final challenge to God by resting on it:

> Let me be weighed in an even balance,
> That God may know mine integrity. (31.6)

These are the last uses of the word in the book, except that in this respect as in others Elihu provides an intellectual and emotional bridge to the voice from the whirlwind by twice associating the word *tam* (36.4, 37.16) with God Himself.

The frame tale rounds out the simpler proof of Job's integrity, but the verse drama complements it and expands it by demonstrating that in another, deeper sense—a sense that linguistically at least, because of the verse, we may call poetic—the integrity is unprovable. Not in itself is the integrity unprovable, but in its relation, the essential relation, to the Creator whose majesty most transcendentally appears precisely when this very question is opened.

It is the same Job who renders a flurry of interrelated assertions and appeals to his friends and to God, under the same pressure. For the speeches of this drama, each transition comes about in response to a silent pressure. A speech ends, and evokes a further speech in the cycle, the more freely in response to pressure from within that there is no demonstrable pressure from without, other than an obscure conventional successiveness, to determine who will speak. Nothing but Job's integrity confronts them, since the ritual has taken care of his sufferings. The friends themselves only carry over in the main transition from silent sympathy after Job himself has broken their seven days of silence. The full weight of those seven days has been needed to propel them into confrontation:

> So they sat down with him upon the ground seven days and seven nights, and none spake a word unto him: for they saw that *his* grief was very great. After this opened Job his mouth, and cursed his day. (2.13-3.1)

The intensification of the friends' speeches once they do speak, is in answer to Job's first utterance, which would simply withdraw from the question entirely. He leaves his self-deprecation for self-justification only as they work their initial mildness into a full reproach that would take the easy way out of the impasse by denying his integrity.

Job, in the responsive cycle of speeches, gets pushed deeper into what he himself calls his bitterness, an ineffectual bitterness. "He poureth out my gall [*mererathi*, 'my bitterness'] upon the ground." (16.13) To say so sinks him further in bitterness, but, under a continuing accusation that surfaces again, "the Almighty has made my soul bitter" (*Shaddai* hemar *naphshi*, 27.2; K.J. "the Almighty, *who* hath vexed my soul").

The answer Job comes to demand from his "adversary" arises, in the dramatic delay of fulfillment, not first from God, but from Elihu, who by his own indirection prepares for the imaged, resumptive indirection of God's final reply. So he will justify an integrity that no process like man-made law, though Job use legal language, can justify, or not justify. Echoing the friends as well as Job, Elihu hits Job's legal points by a somewhat evasive contradiction of the central question:

> He preserveth not the life of the wicked:
> But giveth right to the poor.
> He withdraweth not his eyes from the righteous: (36.6-7)

As though to assert that whatever else can be said, this at least can be said.

Job's breadth of expression forces the friends to try to match him if they are to get through to him, to persuade him to move aside from the impasse. Instead of moving him, their speeches merely expand under the attraction of his own. Eliphaz, for example, contradicts himself by claiming a base of wisdom within men, and then urging the iniquity of man:

> Should a wise man utter vain knowledge . . .? (15.2)
> How much more abominable and filthy
> *Is* man, which drinketh iniquity like water? (15.16)

Moreover, his next statement, by revulsion from his own stand but in imitation of Job's contagious assertiveness, moves ahead into the larger view:

> I will shew thee, hear me;
> And that *which* I have seen I will declare; (15.17)

The word for *see* utilizes the word for *vision, ḥazah*. Eliphaz soon broaches the visionary strain of a prophetic hyperbole to provide an image that sees Job in a majestic way, making him the more exemplary that Eliphaz shifts to the third person:

> Which wise men have told
> From their fathers, . . . (18)
> The wicked man . . . (20)
> . . . wandereth abroad for bread, *saying* Where *is it?*
> He knoweth that the day of darkness is ready at his hand.
> Trouble and anguish shall make him afraid;
> They shall prevail against him, as a king ready to the battle.
> For he stretcheth out his hand against God,
> And strengtheneth himself against the Almighty. (15.23-25)

Thus the very persistence of Job's integrity is turned against him. Capitulation to the friends' limiting emphasis cannot provide relief for Job, nor will the Almighty give him the justification (*tsadaq*) he keeps demanding under the conditions of a human tribunal's limited framework. Job can only identify himself into the totality of his plight. Thereby he gains not release but a clear confrontation of the central mystery, the majesty to which he is rising by first refusing to "curse God and die." Next, when he does "curse" (3.1), he has begun the effort of turning his spirit heroically up out of his desolation from a past that made him prosperous in wealth and offspring, away from the wretched present of itching boils, nakedness, and utter degradation, into the force of the primal questions his plight raises. He rises to the Almighty by steadfastly raising these primal questions. He, the man who plumbs his own worthlessness, also maintains his integrity and sustains this cosmic drama. So, like a root in its growth, he shows at once inward probing and outward thrust. "The root of the thing is found in me."

EMOTION

"Integrity" is the repeated, unifying expression for that in Job which constitutes his justification. As a single term it is somewhat static, and the prose tale attributes the quality to him in a summary, static way. In the verse drama, however, he subjects his integrity to a dynamic process of intellectual and emotional articulation.

Language frames thought, and except under extraordinary conditions the framing of thought occurs along with, and in accordance with, emotion. Psychologists find it possible by several systems to translate emotion into thought, thought into emotion. Moreover, language itself, the medium for expressing emotion and thought, embodies the two in its single words, to begin with, and in its syntax.

Most words carry some emotional tinge as well as an intellectual signification. In the patterns of syntax—the kinds of organization the words undergo—and in the very fact that they are uttered, an emotional sequence can be read, in addition to, or rather indistinguishably from, whatever patterned signification is presented.

Verse heightens the emotional component of a linguistic statement by adding to it a charge of gratuitous recurrence. And scripture further heightens the charge by announcing, in effect, that the context of the utterance is in some way directed toward a divine being.

The utterances of Job, and the friends' responses, are all directed ultimately to God. Immediately they are directed to a sequence not of actions but of confrontations before a cosmic question, one that by being unanswerable, generates more confrontations. In this drama, then, "character" as such emerges as the complex of responses to the central question of man's existence: why pain co-exists with so great a possibility of joy. The responses are verbal responses. And the emotions imperiously demand the reaction of verbal expression. It is of emotion that Eliphaz speaks at the beginning of his first answer to Job:

> *If* we assay to commune with thee, wilt thou be grieved?
> But who can withhold himself from speaking? (4.2)

And later Job says he would die if he could not speak:

> For now, if I hold my tongue, I shall give up the ghost. (13.19)

The friends have made small, silent gestures before the speeches; "mourn" (*nudh*), in "they had made an appointment together to come to mourn with him, and to comfort him," (2.11) signifies the gesture of nodding the head.[5] But the gestures of another drama have been omitted here, and the full course of interaction is carried by the statements.

Job, through the inner complexity of his running expression, exhibits a large capacity to connect one whole emotion with a bigger one, or with its seeming opposite, by moving in association from the first to the second. He goes from a sense of integrity quickly to a sense of degradation and insignificance, from a responsive participation in the world of light and dark to an alienation out of it, from intellectual coherence to an emotional instability that is its other face as well as its opposite. The words constitute the phenomenological nodes of dynamic feeling. They are its irreducible atoms, at once graphing and evoking the complex of thought and emotion. To move from extreme courage to extreme fear, extreme sorrow to extreme joy, extreme awareness of pain to a savoring of visionary pleasure, is to imply the spiritual vastness of a being who can compass these extremes in the flow of his utterance.

Job's integral wholeness is to be seen in his very capacity for psychological swirl from one seemingly partial mood to another. Such a person is to be found elsewhere in Scripture too: in Jeremiah, who expands his predominant sorrow into joy; in Isaiah, who expands his predominant joy into sorrow ("the oil of joy for mourning"), and in the typologically common worshipper figured under the communal "I" of Psalms. Psalm 22, for example, moves out of an initial dejection like Job's:

My God, my God, why hast thou forsaken me?
Why art thou so far from helping me, *and from* the words of my roaring?
O my God, I cry in the daytime, but thou hearest not;
And in the night season, and am not silent. (Ps. 22.1-2)

Through the graphic enumeration of sufferings, the Psalm works its way up to a satisfied praise, and at the end the speaker utters a feeling of Abraham-like attentiveness:

> A seed shall serve him;
> It shall be accounted to the Lord for a generation.
> They shall come, and shall declare his righteousness
> Unto a people that shall be born, that he hath done *this*. (30-31)

The transition from dejection to visionary satisfaction does not take place through any reasoning, except the identifications implied in the verse form of parallelism. Nor is there any proportionate disposition of stanzaic or strophic elements to govern and order the range of feeling. Rather, the formal adaptability of this Psalm and many others creates a sense of what they are drawing on, an orbit of emotion so cosmically and internally God-centered, that joy, perpetually associable to the divine protection, can slip, through an instantaneous, prayerful, verbal change, into a sorrow that bemoans either the speaker's sin toward God or his loss of the divine favor, a loss the very existence of the Psalm declares is hopefully momentary.

The psyche poeticized in Psalms opens as a vast internal weather-chamber of devout moods-becoming-definitions, themselves thereby becoming other moods. Under the dynamic of this possibility, no one mood can totally dominate, and any one mood testifies to a range beyond itself: "Thou hast set my feet in a large room," (Psalms 31.8b), "Thou hast turned for me my mourning into dancing"

(30.11a), "Unless thy law *had been* my delights, I should then have perished in mine affliction" (119.92).

"Law" (*torah*, from *yarah*, teach, instruct), may here imply a process. Under this expansive "law," the verbal stream of consciousness becomes a stream of adaptive prayer, and one of pluralized feeling: "delights." Characteristically, in Psalms the mood alters at once under the impulse of spirit. So the big change from dejection to praise in Psalm 22 operates through the parallelism of a single verse:

> Save me from the lion's mouth:
> For thou hast heard me from the horns of the unicorns.
> (22.21)

The first line here stands in antithesis to the second, if one takes the first for culminating an unrelieved series of dejected statements (1-20) and the second for initiating a hope, based on memory, of an invoked prior aid. In form, though, the parallelism is not antithetical, but synonymous or causal. "Save me" hinges on "thou hast heard me"; "from the lion's mouth" parallels "from the horns of the unicorns." It is only in mood that these verses are antithetical, and yet the mood is all. The hopeful mood, once stated, takes over the rest of the Psalm. The memory, "thou hast heard me," once invoked, becomes a promise in the very next verse:

> I will declare thy name unto my brethren:
> In the midst of the congregation will I praise thee.
> (22.22)

This promise is here being fulfilled in the act of being made, and still more explicitly in the next verse:

> Ye that fear the Lord, praise him. (22.23)

In Job this internal psychological range is given not to the generalized soul, or to the congregation under the figure of the soul, as in Psalms, but rather to distinct persons in a totally demanding and specific (hypothetical) situation. The poetry reflects the internality of a language in which the word *levav,* usually translated "heart," also refers to the mind, and in fact to a human interior that fuses both emotion and thought. The speeches are set up as suasive arguments, but they derive their tendentiousness not so deeply from their logic as from the powerful course of the dynamically adaptive feelings that take shape verse by verse. Zophar, never able to forget the very sympathy that brought him a long distance to spend day after day at the side of his suffering friend, may begin a speech by scolding Job:

> Should thy lies make men hold their peace?
> And when thou mockest, shall no man make thee ashamed?
> (11.3)

This does not mean that his own praise of divine wisdom will not soon bring him round to voice for Job a "hope" (*tiqvah*) that would be contradictory only if we were to imagine him to be subjected to some tighter, merely logical, consistency:

> Because thou shalt forget *thy* misery,
> *And* remember *it* as waters *that* pass away:
> And *thine* age shall be clearer than the noonday;
> Thou shalt shine forth, thou shalt be as the morning.
> And thou shalt be secure, because there is hope.
> (11.16-18a)

Job himself, in his greater disturbance, ranges still more powerfully in his own arguments. There is an emotive break, hopeful rather than confused, in his last summing up:

> Did I fear a great multitude,
> Or did the contempt of families terrify me,
> That I kept silence, *and* went not out of the door? (31.34)
> Oh that one would hear me!
> Behold my desire *is, that* the Almighty would answer me,
> And *that* mine adversary had written a book. (35)
> Surely I would take it upon my shoulder,
> *And* bind it *as* a crown to me. (36)

The break in syntax, from the question of verse 34[6] to the sighing exclamation of verse 35, constitutes a break in emotion from something like righteous indignation to something like a weary appeal, the certitude of the first merging into the uncertainty of the second. The declaration recovers to assert a conditional act of certainty in verse 36. If Job were as justified as he declares in the question of verse 34, why would it be a question? And why could he move on to the demand of 35? The antithesis underlying these verses may be felt between the content and the syntactic form of each unit, as well as in the juxtaposition of units, dynamically complicating the expressed emotion. Moreover, the change of elements in the parallel phrasing (*Multitude* to *families* to *door* to *desire* to *book* to *shoulder* to *crown*) itself serves an emotional expansion so strenuously adaptive as to be gathering itself for a final act of sympathetic imagination. In this act, some shade of complaint still remains. The word "crown" (*'aṭaroth*) recalls its earlier occurrence, contrasted to this one. Job can now set a crown on his head because it was bared of one ("He hath stripped me of my glory, and taken the crown *from* my head," 19.9).

The main dramatic movement in Job follows this spiritual dynamic as it emerges in expressed emotion. It does not simply produce the logical arguments that the commentators strain to reconcile into a nonexistent order of progressive reason. Characteristically a speaker's disposition qualifies what he is saying, sometimes explicitly, as when what is implied by the act of saying may flatly contradict what is said:

> Hold your peace, let me alone, that I may speak,
> And let come on me what *will*.
> Wherefore do I take my flesh in my teeth,
> And put my life in mine hand? (13.13-14)

Job's very stance answers this question. Moreover, being involved in speaking provides him with an adaptively phrased emotion that puts him squarely beyond it:

> Though he slay me, yet will I trust in him. (13.15)[7]

Job suddenly switches here, in the first quotation, from urging a pious silence on his friends to asking how he himself can be so bold as to speak. But the act of speaking, if bold, would then be defining itself as more dangerous than the silence (which Job had broken to urge his friends on). He drops this contradiction in the next verse, the first half of which asserts, by countervailing emotions, the utmost of piety, while the second half goes on in stoutly maintained self-assertion:

> Though he slay me, yet will I trust in him:
> But I will maintain mine own ways before him. (13.15)

The emotions stay out in the open by their reactions, for the friends react at once to every turn of Job, as he to theirs:

> For *it is* evident unto you if I lie.
> [Literally, "It is on your faces if I lie."] (6.28b)

He can read their reactions "on your faces" (*'al panekhem*).

The very situation renders him subject to the sway of this internal range of emotion. As Fohrer[8] says, the theme is not "abstract" on Job's side but "concrete," a human existence in suffering. Or, as Westerman[9] puts it, "Existence asks something else . . . Why must I suffer . . . ?" "This question does not come about in such a way that a man thinking about his suffering makes it into an object. This questioning-why comes, rather *directly* [italics Westerman's] out of the suffering . . . It is not a discussion but a contending-conversation [*Streitgespräch*]." And, as he goes on to say, the "*Streitgespräch*" allows the dialogue a range and fluidity of expressive forms, "this contending-speech is in no way a distinct form of speaking; much more does it include in itself all the forms."

The voice of each involved speaker is free to take a leap in a direction of newly parallel relation to what he has just said. The strength of the verbalized emotions leads each speaker to keep exercising that freedom anew. Consequently, the emotional link, from verse to verse, determines the dramatistic progressions in Job, first because speech must issue from felt motive to exist at all (everyone begins by being silent for seven whole days, till the feelings reach a certain pitch); and next because the specific direction taken by the intellectual associations of paralleling utterance are at every point determined by a momentarily predominant feeling:

> Lo, mine eye hath seen all *this*,
> Mine ear hath heard and understood it. (13.1)
> What ye know, *the same* do I know also:
> I *am* not inferior to you. (2)
> Surely I would speak to the Almighty,
> And I desire to reason with God. (3)
> But ye *are* forgers of lies,
> Ye *are* all physicians of no value. (4)
> Oh that ye would altogether hold your peace!
> And it should be your wisdom. (5)
> Hear now my reasoning,
> And hearken to the pleadings of my lips. (6)
> Will ye speak wickedly for God?
> And talk deceitfully for him? (7)
> Will ye accept his person?
> Will ye contend for God? (8)
> Is it good that he should search you out?
> Or as one man mocketh another, do ye *so* mock him? (9)
> He will surely reprove you,
> If ye do secretly accept persons. (10)

Realizing his own perception (1), leads Job to try once more to rise out of his dejectedness by declaring his equality to the friends (2). His sense of this immediately (3) exalts him to where he would asseverate ("surely": *'ulam*, "only") the desire to speak—nay, to "reason" (*hokheaḥ*, contend) with God. From the elevation of this desire he turns back with increased scorn to the friends who "plaster falsehood" (4, literally); whose speaking is not only false but useless as a remedy; they are "healers of vanity." For them to be so makes them not only useless; saying so makes him realize, in his feelings, that they are also a positive plague; and this emotional response leads him to utter another desire, that they would be still. But, having expressed the wish to silence them, he does not wish to drive them away; and his next statement (6), given in the imperative which the ascendancy of the above emotional sequence (1-6) allows him to assume, bids them (rather than God) to listen to his "reasoning." The same root *thokhaḥti* he has used in verse 3 now assumes somewhat more strongly the notion of contention, since it stands in parallelism to "pleading," where above it had merely paralleled "speak." For the next four verses (7-10) he dwells on what would happen if the friends were to take a false position (as they are doing; but the rhetorical questions characteristically leave both possibilities open) toward God, excluding them (9) from speaking with God as he himself would have done. Now the repeated verb *hokheaḥ* takes on fully the sense of advocacy against the friends, as Job's feelings come to a head in the Hebrew idiom of iterating a word for emphasis (*hokheah yokhiaḥ* (10) "will surely reprove"). As this verb is driven through its changes, so every one of Job's responses, point for point, has been evoked by the logic of emotional reaction, up to a statement that the parallelism itself gives the strength of repetition. The principle of linkages from one statement to another is found in the dominant feeling. One particular logical association is chosen among other possible ones through the situational direction of emotion. The emotional force that each man constantly exemplifies when he speaks allows for the possibility of associative freedom, but also for self-entrapment.

This emotional force, this inner "quaking," (*roghez*) characterizes man as much as does his shortness of life, Job says soon in another long turn of the same speech:

> Man *that is* born of a woman
> *Is* of few days, and full of trouble. (14.1)
> [*sheva' roghez:* literally "teeming with turbulence" or
> "satiated with quaking"]

It is indeed "out of the whirlwind" that God himself speaks to Job, the text twice says (38.1; 40.6).

Reacting to their own emotions from within the "quaking" of their own depths, the friends are reacting to one another. And this happens through Job, once he gets beyond the "curse" of his first speech, something that the concerned gentleness of Eliphaz's first

LIBRARY ST. MARY'S COLLEGE

answer has inspired him to do. Eliphaz himself strives to counterbalance Job's nearly unrelieved despair, wherein the "turbulence" keeps leading him to repeat the same wish to die. Eliphaz' feeling of sympathy keeps him holding out against his friend's dejection. As he says to Job:

> Thy words have upholden him that was falling,
> And thou hast strengthened the feeble knees. (4.4)

Should not Job be using his old virtue to bring himself out of the slump? In asking this, Eliphaz cannot change the fact that his friend sits suffering on the dungheap. Perhaps Job's unresponsiveness, together with his own fatigue, and a frustration that seven days of ritual silence spent at Job's side have failed to console him, induce Eliphaz to modify his gentleness. Hence, perhaps, he comes out with what is uppermost in his mind, an indirect version of the thought that Job must have done something to alter an earlier virtue:

> But now it is come upon thee, and thou faintest;
> It toucheth thee, and thou art troubled. (4.5)

And soon the indirectness is dropped:

> Remember, I pray thee, who *ever* perished, being innocent?
> Or where were the righteous cut off? (4.7)

This thought grips his emotions enough to dominate him for the rest of his speech, in a crescendo of terrified reaction ("the hair of my flesh stood up" 4.15b). All men, his fear brings him to think, may be unstable:

> Behold, he put no trust in his servants;
> And his angels he charged with folly:
> How much less *in* them that dwell in houses of clay,
> Whose foundation *is* in the dust,
> *Which* are crushed before the moth? (4.18-19)

The same word for "foundation(s)," *yesodham,* will imply a different feeling when in the mouth of God:

> Where wast thou when I laid the foundations of the earth?
> (38.4a)

"Earth" elsewhere, in fact, is expressed by "dust": in 14.8, and also here in 5.6:

> Although affliction cometh not forth of the dust,
> Neither doth trouble spring out of the ground. . . .

Eliphaz generalizes the notion of trouble:

> Yet man is born unto trouble,
> As the sparks fly upward. (5.7)

And immediately thereupon, as though inwardly relieved at the possibility at least of formulating affliction, he proposes to Job what will become the actual course of behavior Job will talk himself into adopting:

> I would seek unto God,
> And unto God would I commit my cause. (5.8)

God is so great indeed (5.8-15) that the deprived and the unjust alike should act appropriately toward him (Eliphaz does not specify in what category he is placing Job):

> So the poor hath hope,
> And iniquity stoppeth her mouth.
> Behold, happy *is* the man whom God correcteth:
> Therefore despise not thou the chastening of the Almighty:
> (5.16-17)

But Job does not respond as Eliphaz would be relieved to see him respond, because Eliphaz is mainly hearkening to his own dynamic of desire, consoling himself more than his friend. The strands in his argument are flexible to the enchainment of a feeling more concerned with resolving its own perplexity than in coming fully to terms with what it means for Job to suffer.

The emotional intensity, here and throughout, keeps impregnating the thought. The unconscious element, indeed, finds toward the end an explicit delineation:

> In a dream, in a vision of the night,
> When deep sleep falleth upon men

In slumberings upon the bed;
Then he openeth the ears of men,
And sealeth their instruction,
That he may withdraw man *from his* purpose,
And hide pride from man. (33.15-17)

And often the emotion intensifies its own references:

If I have withheld the poor from *their* desire,
Or have caused the eyes of the widow to fail; (31.16)

Job is here condensing the psycho-spiritual interdependence of thought and emotion. In a conditional sentence mainly asserting his own righteousness, he is implying a rebuke to the comforters that their eyes are failing, as those of older women (they have declared the wisdom of old *men*) tend to do. He is implying, too, a determination that his own eyes shall not fail, as well as perhaps also a fear that they may be failing because he is near the end of his days, or because in his affliction he cannot see far enough to resolve his perplexity. To feel so, however, is bringing him all the time to see farther, far enough to let emotion, in its spiritual resolution, triumph, where mere thought must remain perplexed.

PARALLELISM

The form of the verse in Job, to begin with, casts all utterances into a pattern that coordinates their assertions. The "thought-rhyme" or parallelism of Hebrew verse has just one rule: the second half of a verse must in some way repeat what was said in the first half. This simply doubling form permits a range of poetic identities and contrasts. So Job, directly in a couplet or indirectly in a longer repetition, can simultaneously worship God and blame him:

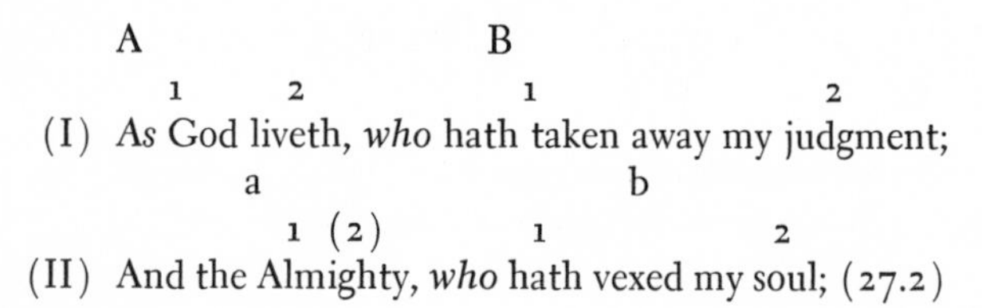

	a			b	
	1	2		1	2
	ḥay'el			hesir	mishpaṭi
	Live	God		taking-away	my-judgment
		1	(2)	1	2
ve	shaddai			hemar	naphshi
And	Almighty			embittering	my-soul

The first interjection swears by God (A); the second (B) part, in the expectation of the parallelism, turns out not to repeat it simply, or even by the mere contradiction of what is called, rather roughly, "antithetical parallelism." B alters A dynamically, by defining the God who should "live" not by a synonym or syntactic equivalent of the third person imperative "live," but by a causative participle (*hesir,* causative active participle of *sur,* "remove"). This verb calls the "Lord" (*'el*), a "taker-away" of "my judgment." So it asserts that he violates the juridical principle which would deal fairly with Job and prove the God alive whom his oath has just proclaimed to be alive. And prove Job alive too; "my judgment" parallels "my soul," and the word *nephesh* means also "breath of life." In the second half of the line Job repeats God's name with the paralleling variation of a stronger term, *Shaddai,* the Almighty, that reference to an omnipotent creative principle which recurs in Job as a divine name more frequently than in all the other books of the Old Testament together. "The Almighty," however, has acted in a way that repeats the complaint of the first half-line, and "taker-away" is paralleled by "embittering" (*hemar,* causative participle of *marar*), though the action is no longer external, but internal, affecting the very "soul" of Job. *Nephesh,* "soul," also may mean "life," and therefore, in a sense, it completes the circle by paralleling the very first word of the verse, "*ḥay,*" live.

The structure of the verse itself, then, contains the possibility of many implied assertions. The contradictions built into it are overcome by the total affirmation of Job's resurgent feeling, which stamps the very words of complaint by the counterbalancing verse of prayer and praise, "Live the Lord." Within the logical thought-rhyme of the parallelism, the statement is held implicitly in a perpetual framework of equivalences. And when something other than equivalence—as here, a contradiction; or an image ("emblematic parallelism"), or a rising series of repetitions ("staircase parallelism") —bursts into the verse, the new element is still held, through the pairing of the verse form, either as a kind of submerged equivalence, or also as the redirection of an equivalence the thought-rhyme leads us to expect. Statement (I) at least reaffirms Statement (II) ("God . . . hath taken away my judgment," about equals "The Almighty . . . hath vexed my soul"). The parallel elements of word or syntax may introduce a qualification that is always superimposed on the base of equivalence ("taker-away" expands and opposes "live"; "soul" expands "judgment"; "embittering" extends "taker-away"). In the form that his words must have if he speaks a Hebrew verse, Job struggles to contain his complaint in an attitude of adoration, as the rabbi Rashi[10] comments on this passage, "It is an oath, for in truth He hath taken away my judgment; and from this judgment Joshua expounded that out of love Job served the Omnipresent God, because no man makes a vow by the life of the king unless he loves the king." In the tensions of a verse form as simple as the base of grammatical predication itself, Job manages to encoil contradictions his very stance proves he is transcending.

Parallelism poeticizes the act of predication by displacing it into a twinned syntactic unit. To say "A is B," then "a is b," and match A with a and B with b, has the effect of qualifying the initially paired predication by two others, one for each member of the first. A formal, paratactically equalized pairing, sets the first half of a line into relation with the second, by involving identifications among members of the two halves in a process comparable to the one through which the statement of either half must be made, the normal process of syntax. To use Jakobson's terms,[11] the axis of selection (A matches a) is brought into rapport with the axis of combination (A is B) by recourse to the poetic convention of parallelism rather than through other means. Since logical statements must proceed by some kind of predication, the logical skeleton, or what amounts to it at a time before formal philosophy existed, is at once made paramount. At the same time, because it is altered and paired, the bare predication is given a sense of improvisatory arbitrariness. Reasoning from the universality of predication attributable to any syntax in a human language, some have thought the duality involved in predication to be an intrinsic attribute of the human mind. In Hebrew verse, this duality resides in the line, and triumphs by the virtuosity of gratuitous repetition. Such pairings, again, provide the halves for the kind of axes of binary symbolic equivalences or oppositions upon which an anthropologist like Lévi-Strauss can order well-nigh all societal phenomena into isomorphic equilibrium.

Though the parallelism must carry in some form from one half of the verse to the other, the fact that it often carries further, and that its modes of repetition vary, makes its boundary uncertain. To continue a parallel element, then, stands as an omnipresent possibility at every point in a stretch of Hebrew verse. And just within the bound of the single whole verse where parallelism must apply, at least four interlocking predications are set up: A is B (1); a is b (2); A is a (3); and B is b (4). These possibilities increase when, as often in Job, the elements in a distich are tripled (A, B, C; a, b, c). Among the identities and contrarieties of just four, any one can be made to equal, or in a variable degree to qualify, the other three. Thereby any one part can dominate any congeries of the three other parts, or be dominated by them, in the proto-philosophic simplicities of pregnant statement. In Job, therefore, the form allows any one angle of the situation to dominate, in the indeterminacy of paralleling succession. *Though he slay me, yet will I trust in him* (13.15),[12] a paradox in its syntactic form, is something more than a paradox if the second part be taken for some kind of corollary to the first. There is no Hebrew word for "though," only the exclamatory *hen*, "behold": "Behold he slay me, in him I trust." Moreover, if both parts are seen as in formally stated duplication with a circle of verses around them, then the circle may be widened increasingly (to include, as parallel to "slay," for example, all the meditations on human mortality in the book) until the boundary of the book be reached.

Taken as a series of logical and syntactic statements, the parallelisms multiply identities, or at least equivalences, up to the maximum paratactic point of equalling all of one saying with all of another. Taken as a poetic expression, these multiplications exemplify the "gratuitous" character of poetic language by saying everything double, and therefore by calling attention to the component of inventive variation in saying it either time. Instead of just moving freely ahead, the verse doubles back to prove that a statement can be said a different way, and to show that the first way of saying it was put as arbitrarily as the second. In the seriousness of Scripture what results is not an impression of aesthetic play, but an increase in the freedom of range for the expression of sacred utterance. Religiosity, in all styles, tends to amplify the range of linguistic expression: Luther's Bible, the King James Version, the prose of Newman or Kierkegaard or St. Augustine, all receive some heightening of pitch just from their concerns. And in the verse style of scripture, as Bishop Lowth says about sacred Hebrew poetry, a sublimity inheres in the very simplicity of the utterance,[13] a simplicity that cannot readily be discussed in any normal category of "high" or "low" or "middle" style, at least partly because the verse style rests on so single a convention, that of the statement doubled in parallelism.

The dynamism of change in this verse operates too subtly and too complexly for the categories of type classification which Lowth and others have employed in a taxonomy of analysis that must be taken as preliminary. An image in the second half of a verse may be called "emblematic" parallelism; and yet often, as in the precious metals and stones paraded by Chapter 28 of Job, the images act primarily as aphoristic instances. They are only secondarily emblems of wisdom, and then *a fortiori:* silver is precious (and hard to find, but men find it), wisdom is even more precious (and harder to find; how shall it be found?). The structure of "x is less than y" may also be taken as a subtype of "antithetical parallelism," and the fact that the verse dwells for so long on one kind of image may be called "staircase parallelism," the extension of a parallel element for longer than a verse or two. Yet the verse tends everywhere to dwell on similar statements, to circle back on a unitary condition of which any given verse is only an aspect. Consequently, the progression of verses may, from one point of view, always be taken for a "staircase," as the basic parallelism of Lowth, "synonymous" parallelism, under his very definition, only offers a maximum state for a condition everywhere present in the verse. That Job brings so long and coherent a series of verses as Chapter 28[14] into such relatively simple identification, signifies in itself a majestic pause for his upwelling optimism. Yet even there the dynamism of identifications spreading through the verses and beyond to other speeches is strongly, if quietly, at work.

This is true of the overall momentary theme: "Treasure is great but wisdom is greater" gets swept up in, and sublimely anticipates, the final affirmations of God in Chapter 38, "Divine wisdom is greater superlatively, in that it can create not only 'treasures . . . of the snow' and 'of the hail,' (38.22), but 'wisdom' and 'understanding' themselves" (38.36). The force of this transcendent conclusion renders these earlier emblems of treasure not only "less than" wisdom, but "greater than," in so far as they provide instances of the overwhelming wonder of the Creator's creation. Instances are something less than emblems, and also something existentially more.

Job is especially remarkable for its vividly concrete images. These work, even more remarkably, at once as instances of the point under discussion and as surfacing instances, gradually paralleling other instances, of the ordered magnificence in God's Creation. The dynamic movement in which the images partake, supersedes the momentary structure of simile or metaphor. "And under it is turned up as it were fire," (28.5b); "as the sparks [literally "sons of flame"] fly upward" (5.7); "the flame shall dry up his branches" (15.30)—

it is incidental that grammatically the first is a simile, the second a simile imbedding a metaphor, and the third a literal statement. There comes through first the succinct vividness of each fire image, and then the logical tension of each as it parallels the images of light throughout.

And characteristically, the multiple references work far and wide through the book. The first here, in referring to the interior of the earth, also parallels Job's images of interiority; those of "children" are paralleled by the second; the motif of "destruction of vegetation" by the third; and "unpredictable violent action" by all three.

A close inspection of Chapter 28 will show how elaborately these multiple references are constructed. For all this chapter's state of relative rest, in it the larger dynamism of the whole is served by the constant motions of smaller dynamisms through the associative patterns that the very form of the verse offers. The parallel verses point for point extend and link the senses of each verse, and without ambiguity. (The numbers placed above the letters in this passage indicate elements that can be classified together as parallel beyond a given verse. The fairly regular tripartite parallelism I have marked A, B, C, setting up the first hemistich of each verse according to the Hebrew sequence, and then marking it above the English):

(1) (1+2+x+y) (3)
A | C | B
Surely there is | a vein | for the silver,
ki yesh | | la keseph motsa'

(2) (3) (2+x)
a | b | c
and a place | for gold | where they fine *it*. 1
u maqom | la zahav | yazoqqu

(3) (2+x+y) (2+1)
A | C | B
Iron | is taken | out of the earth,
barzel | | me'aphar yuqqaḥ

(3) (2+x+y) (2+1+6)
a c b
and brass *is* molten *out of* the stone. 2
ve 'even yatsuq neḥushah

(4+2+x) (5) (7)
B A C
He setteth an end to darkness,
qets sam le ḥoshek u le

(4+2+x) (5+8) (8+9+7)
B A C
and searcheth out all perfection:
khol takhlith hu' ḥoqer

(6) (2+7) (2+7)
C C_2 C
the stones of darkness, and the shadow of death. 3
even 'ophel ve tsalmaveth

(10+2) (2+4+11+x+y) (2+12)
B A C
The flood breaketh out from the inhabitant;
paratz naḥal me'im gar

(1+2+7+13) (11+14)
(a+b) c
even the waters forgotten of the foot:
ha nnishkaḥim minni-raghel

(2+10+13+15+x) (2+10+13) (12)
a (a+b) c
they are dried up, they are gone away from men. 4
dallu me'enosh na'u

1+2 (2+x) (y+16)
A B C
As for the earth, out of it cometh bread:
erets mimmennah yetse' laḥem

2 (2+x+y) (1+17)
a b c
and under it is turned up as it were fire. 5
ve thaḥteha nehpak kemo 'esh

LIBRARY ST. MARY'S COLLEGE

(2+6) C | (2) A | (3+19) B
The stones of it | *are* the place | of sapphires:
meqom sapir 'avaneha

(1) c | (2) a | (3) b
and it hath | dust | of gold. 6
ve 'aphroth zahav lo

(2+7+14) A | (20) B | (4+13+21) C
There is a path | which no fowl | knoweth,

(20) b | (18+22) b | (4+13+22) c
and which the vulture's | eye | hath not seen: 7

22+23 | 7+13+14+x
The lion's whelps | have not trodden it,

11+13+20 x+13
nor the fierce lion passed by it. 8

He putteth forth his hand upon the rock;
He overturneth the mountains by the [ḥallamish, flint] roots. 9
He cutteth out rivers among the rocks;
And his eye seeth every precious thing. 10
He bindeth the floods from overflowing;
And *the thing that is* hid bringeth he forth to light [*yotsi'*]. 11
But where shall wisdom be found?
And where *is* the place of understanding? 12
Man knoweth not the price thereof;
Neither is it found in the land of the living. 13
The depth saith, It *is* not in me:
And the sea saith, *It is* not with me. 14
It cannot be gotten for gold,
Neither shall silver be weighed *for* the price thereof. 15
It cannot be valued with the gold of Ophir,
With the precious onyx, or the sapphire. 16
The gold and the crystal cannot equal it:
And the exchange of it *shall not be for* jewels of fine gold. 17
No mention shall be made of coral, or of pearls:
For the price of wisdom *is* above rubies. 18

The topaz of Ethiopia shall not equal it,
Neither shall it be valued with pure gold. 19
Whence then cometh wisdom?
And where *is* the place of understanding? 20
Seeing it is hid from the eyes of all living,
And kept close from the fowls of the air. 21
Destruction and death say,
We have heard the fame thereof with our ears. 22
God understandeth the way thereof,
And he knoweth the place thereof. 23
For he looketh to the ends of the earth,
And seeth under the whole heaven; 24
To make the weight for the winds;
And he weigheth the waters by measure. 25
When he made a decree for the rain,
And a way for the lightning of the thunder; 26
Then did he see it, and declare it;
He prepared it, yea, and searched it out. 27
And unto man he said,
Behold, the fear of the Lord, that *is* wisdom;
And to depart from evil *is* understanding. 28

Beyond the overall double antithesis of comparison, question, and answer, there is at work in these verses a profound movement toward verbal and spiritual identifications. Just with regard to sense (and there are also rhythmic echoes throughout), a word carries facets which get reflected throughout by partial parallel variations, the other senses of the same word reflecting still others in turn.

The categories in some cases call for an arbitrary extension, in other cases for an arbitrary restriction, since one could classify all under somewhat more general headings, much as I have done with those I have lettered *x* and *y*. In the listing below, the correspondences in verses 1-8 are marked above, over the verses themselves. The equivalent ones to be found in verses 9-25 are listed here. These are, then, the categories:

x) *verb of action:* verses 9-11, begotten, cometh

y) *motion out of:* putteth forth, overflowing, bring forth to light, whence cometh, depart from, search out

1) *assertion, place:* where . . . be found, where . . . place, be found, is it found, land, depth, it is not (twice), whence, place, place thereof, declare, behold
2) *earth, interior:* rock, mountain, roots, rocks, thing that is hid. Land, depths, it is hid, ends of the earth, searched out
3) *precious metal, base metal:* precious thing, price, gold, silver, gold of Ophir, gold, price, price, pure gold
4) *God, divine action,* verses 9-10: God understandeth, fear of the Lord
5) *limit* (related to 8 and 9): (-) overflowing
6) *stone* (opposite to 16; like 3 and 19): rock (flint), mountain, rocks, crystal
7) *darkness* (opposite to 18): depth, death
8) *totality* (like 9 and 5): every (precious thing), equal, exchange, all living, whole heaven
9) *completeness* (like 8 and 5): land of the living, ends of the earth
10) *waters* (opposite to 15): rivers, floods, depth, sea, waters, rain, thunder
11) *violent action* (related to *x*) (and *y*): verses 9-10; destruction, winds
12) *inhabitant* (related to 2): man, land of the living, all the living
13) *forget—disappear* (related to 7): verse 9; knoweth not, it is not in, it is not with, hid from
14) *walk, foot* (related to 12) (and *y*): way
15) *dry* (opposite to 10):
16) *bread* (opposite to 6):
17) *fire* (like 18) (and 19): lightning
18) *light* (opposite to 7) to light, lightning, (most of the items in 3)
19) *gem* (like 3) (and 18): onyx, sapphire, crystal, coral, pearls, rubies, topaz
20) *bird/beast* eyes of all living, fowls of the air
21) *know* (classifiable as like 4): wisdom, understanding, knoweth (not), wisdom, understandeth, decree, see, wisdom, understanding

22) *see* (like 18, 21); (opposite to 2), 7); his eye (—) hid from eyes (—) heard the fame
23) *child:*
24) *measure:* bindeth, keep close, weight, weights, make a decree, prepared

I should emphasize that this series is fairly arbitrary and unstructured. The multiple densities of the paralleled elements, and the form of parallelism itself, would especially lend these items to the sort of prolonged, elaborate restructuring into transformations of binary opposition and identity that Claude Lévi-Strauss performs on the much simpler series of South American Indian myths in *Le Cru et le cuit* and *Du Miel aux cendres.*

If we look, then, just at the running identifications, without pausing to restructure them elaborately, there are, to begin with, the simple series, like that of metals and stones (marked "3"), beginning with the conventional Biblical pair, silver and gold. All these are in a kind of antithetical parallelism to Job's "miserable" images. Here he runs through simpler metals, iron and brass, seen not only as useful but as comparable to gold in the wonder of their protective function. He goes on to what vaguely includes these, the "stones" of darkness; stones that are the "place" of the gem that is said (Exodus 24.10) to pave heaven, the sapphire (probably lapis lazuli). For the time, he concludes on gold, in a phrase "dusts of gold" (*'phroth zahav*) which is remarkable for giving the first word in the new periphrasis a plural it receives in only one other place in the Bible (Proverbs 8.26). "Dust" appears as an element in another series of words for the earth or its interior in verse 2a (*'phar* "dust," translated as "earth" for one of its senses in the King James Version). "Dusts" pulverizes "gold" into gold dust as it were, dispersing the precious metal into uniformity with its base source. "Stone" has also gone from singular (*'even,* 2, + 3) to plural (*'avanehah,* 5); and it also shades over from "base" to "precious" in the irrepressible wonderment Job enunciates through this speech. The whole series, reading backward, has come through the "stones" paralleling "dusts" in verse 6.

"Stones" also parallels the "earth" (*'erets*) that firmly opens verse 5. And "earth" may be taken as well to parallel the obscure "flood" of verse 4, since it is connected to the earth's interior by association with the verbs and other words of flowing that are introduced by "molten out of the stone" (*yatsaq*, "pour") in verse 2b. This verbal root had earlier been coupled with the notion of a firmness suggesting that of a hard metal once poured: "thou shalt be steadfast and not fear" 11.15). "Steadfast" translates *mutsaq*, literally "poured out." As Driver[15] says, "the word is often used of the *casting* of metals; and hence, in the passive participle and some derivatives, it appears to have acquired the sense of *firm*." Driver further cites its use in 41.15, in 37.18, "the sky which is strong and as a molten (*mutsaq*) looking glass," and in 38.38, "when the dust groweth into hardness (*mutsaq*)"—all uses that include parallels of other elements in Chapter 28.

The "earth" words go back through the first "stone," through the "place" of verse 1, and take their fountainhead in the capping word of verse 1-a, (*motsa'*). That word, as translated "vein," anticipates the fusion of "dusts of gold" by including both "base" (earth) and "precious," though by concentration and not dispersion. As its open vowel and syntactic position emphasize, *motsa'* is important; and it comprises two further associations of idea to which this speech keeps returning. Meaning literally "an issuing forth," from the verb root *yatsa'* "go forth," this word begins, more generally, the long series of verbs for active processes; "fine," "taken out of," "molten out of," "searcheth out," and so on, a series so dominant in the chapter that I have labelled them *x*. Even more specifically, it implies a "motion out of," itself so recurrent that I have labelled it *y*—a notion which shades into that of the earth and its interior from which the precious metals come.

Both these notions, of active process and of motion out of, relate to another gradually surfacing pair, darkness and light. Light, in turn, connects to "seeing" and then to "understanding" and "wisdom." Even without the stark Biblical word for darkness, "shadow of death" (*tsalmaveth*), this verse asserts its tonic importance and its all-encompassing character by charging the words with multiple interreferences. Light and darkness recur throughout Job in manifold combination, one often metamorphosing into the other (as 17.12; 11.13-17). Just such a change is expressed in an earlier speech of Job, where the same verbal root is used, *yatsa'*, and the same expression for "darkness" is chosen: "[He] bringeth out to light the shadow of death" (*vayyotse' la'or tsalmaveth*, 12.22b).

When *motsa'*[16] is paralleled later in Chapter 28 by the repetition of its actual verb root, it is not to vary any of these four motifs it triumphantly sets out by combining (active process, motion out of, earth's interior, source of precious metal). The root in verse 4b introduces a notion unrelated to these, and to the speech so far, as well as antithetical to all that has been said before, "earth: out of it comes (*yetse'*) . . . bread." And at its next appearance in verse 11, the same verb root makes, and marks, another leap to understanding, "and the hid bringeth he forth (*yotsi'*) to light," by the process of bringing something bright (like a precious metal) out of some interior (hid). Here the term "floods," though it mainly parallels "understanding," may also parallel gold and sapphires for brightness—and just because the two are again paired by verbs of bringing forth, and because "bindeth the floods" is juxtaposed with "bring . . . to light."

The verse form of parallelism makes any repetition, of sense or actual word, more forceful than either an accident or a grace note could be. But the associative dynamism of its progress also keeps the verse from a formal and hierarchized structure. "Light" only touches "understanding," and is not identified with it (or distinguished from it).

The senses of a word provide, then, not just a single duplication for the set parallelism, but several simultaneous ones. And in the forthrightness of expression, there is nothing here that can properly be called ambiguity, unless multiple associativeness be taken for that.

The condensed multiple-facings of "stone" or "vein," or "flood" or "out from," reveal, and exemplify point for point, a state in the speaker of solemn intensity: he can say a great deal in every word. The multiplying process displays the dramatic inner dynamism where a response of anything in the soul, out to its reflection in the cosmos, can be seen to bear integrally on anything else.

All this movement appears microscopically in a given speech. And, as the circle of parallelism widens and the emotion of a speech calls forth sympathy and identification, there is a countlessly altered, but multiple reflection of the same multiple complexes, as well as of single elements; "stone," "water-flood," and "dust" are all three combined differently in an earlier verse:

> The waters wear the stones:
> Thou washest away the things which grow *out* of the dust
> of the earth; (14.19).

Elihu later reflects several of the points of Job's speech in Chapter 28, as he reflects its main bearing:

> Will he esteem thy riches? *no,* not gold
> Nor all the forces of strength.
> Desire not the night,
> When people are cut off in their place.
> Take heed, regard not iniquity:
> For this hast thou chosen rather than affliction.
> Behold, God exalteth by his power:
> Who teacheth like him?
> Who hath enjoined him his way?
> Or who can say, Thou hast wrought iniquity?
> Remember that thou magnify his work,
> Which men behold.
> Every man may see it;
> Man may behold *it* afar off. (36.19-25)

And God's speech gathers up other elements, to realign them:

> Hast thou entered into the springs of the sea?
> Or hast thou walked in search of the depth?
> Have the gates of death been opened unto thee?

> Or hast thou seen the doors of the shadow of death?
> Hast thou perceived the breadth of the earth?
> Declare if thou knowest it all.
> Where *is* the way *where* light dwelleth?
> And *as for* darkness, where *is* the place thereof . . .[17]
> (38.16-19)

In the broadening identity of these statements, it is always possible for a later verse to parallel an earlier one quite closely, as 28.6:

> The stones of it *are* the place of sapphires:
> And it hath dust of gold . . .

parallels 28.16:

> It cannot be valued with the gold of Ophir,
> With the precious onyx, or the sapphire.

Job's speech about wisdom undergoes heightening in the sublime echo-chambers of God's voice:

> Where wast thou when I laid the foundations of the earth?
> Declare if thou hast understanding.
> Who hath laid the measures thereof, if thou knowest?
> Or who hath stretched the line upon it?
> Whereupon are the foundations thereof fastened?
> Or who laid the cornerstone thereof;
> When the morning stars sang together,
> And all the sons of God shouted for joy? . . . (38.4-7)
> Hast thou entered into the treasures of the snow?
> Or hast thou seen the treasures of the hail . . . ? (22)
> By what way is the light parted
> *Which* scattereth the east wind upon the earth?
> Who hath divided a watercourse for the overflowing of waters,
> Or a way for the lightning of thunder . . . ? (24, 25)

Versions of the same ideas underlie Job's speeches and God's: that God's creation, when compared with man's wisdom, resides in mystery (as does wisdom, if compared with riches mysteriously hidden in the earth); that the physical creation itself testifies to God's majesty. The last idea, culminating and also permeating the book, dominates God's speech, while it only erupts into Job's, especially in

28.24-27. Still, these verses closely parallel 38.23-25. The phrase "lightning of thunder" (*ḥaziz qoloth*) is exactly repeated, and the themes of controlling "waters" and distributing precipitation recur here, as elsewhere in these speeches. Verse 25a of God's speech echoes at least three passages of Job's (28.3, 17, and 10). And of the first verses quoted here, every element repeats and recombines elements from Job's speech, except the verbs. These are verbs of action, but measurement and foundation dominate them, not taking something from an interior: the view is transmuted, except for one repetition; the verb *sam* "lay, set." In 38.5 we have the same word, and perhaps the same agent, as in 28.3. The verb is a common one, but the actions are comparable. There God[18] (or man?) "setteth—an end to darkness," and the view is from a point to a limit. Here God sets—"measures" (*memadeah*), the very word used in 28.25, but in the singular there, and with a different perspective. In God's conspectus the view is of perfect order, emanating from a limitless lofty source (the *treasures* of the snow melt when they hit the earth; but they exist permanently, and not in the earth's interior, as do the treasures that Job's speech dwells on).

Job's overall question, "where will wisdom be found" amounts really to an assertion: wisdom is invisible, and so it resembles God. Hence his question anticipates God's questions: "Where were you . . . ?" But Job's questions are put in the negative, pointing to his own bitterness, and yet also to the humility which can get picked up by, and share in, God's splendid affirmations. So Job's bearing, as it defines its own dynamic unity by voicing it, gets redefined as God recombines some particulars of his speech in a comparable rhetorical form, the question. And He goes on to add others; the repetitions of light, treasure, and the rest, elevate into the new affirmation of a singing order of the morning stars and a shouting response, by the joyous sons of God. That also parallels: the phrase, "sons of God," again (*bene 'Elohim*), is taken from the straight prose narrative (1.6; 2.1); the many early repetitions of *bene* tend to parallel Job's sons, 1.5. In the whirlwind speech, "sons of God" is made an element in an act of worship more deeply and wholly responsive than the ritual visits of that first recounting.

Parallelism, then, serves here as a structural rib par excellence, allowing every step to be shown in multiple relation to every other, in the dramatic form of statement and encompassing counterstatement. To speak of sons, *bene,* is to take one of Job's great sufferings, his loss of his children, and obscure it through countering it with an aboriginal act of jubilation by sons. When a speaker remains silent on a recurrent topic, his omission, through the verse form, leaves a blank in the many-dimensioned table of paralleled significances, and the blank carries its own emotional emphasis. Job rarely speaks of children; though in the speech of bitter complaint immediately preceding and counter-evoking the eulogy of Wisdom, he does bring his sons' deaths obliquely into comparison with the fate of a wicked man's sons: (Even if the righteous suffer) the wicked suffer; and wisdom is superior to riches:

> If his children be multiplied *it is* for the sword:
> And his offspring shall not be satisfied with bread. (27.14)

The unsatisfying bread here, of course, stands in a not too distant antithetic parallelism to the good bread that "cometh out of the earth" in 28.5.

In Chapter 28 Job is soon to praise as a human achievement (inadequate only because short of wisdom) the riches he here declares to be useless for the wicked man who will lose his wealth (as the righteous Job lost his):

> Though he heap up silver as the dust,
> And prepare raiment as the clay;
> He may prepare *it,* but the just shall put *it* on,
> And the innocent shall divide the silver. (27.16-17)

All of Chapter 28, in fact, stands in complex antithetical parallelism to Chapter 27. The emotional leap is made from one chapter to the other through a single conjunction preceding the repetition of "silver," the very first word of the chapter, "*ki.*" This is translated "surely," and it does contain such asseveration, strongly enough to shift the flow from vindictiveness about the wicked (27) into praise for the resourcefulness that unearths what the wicked desire (28). But it is a causal word, large enough in its range of meaning to sustain the complex of causal probes which constitutes the center of Job. "Because," "therefore," "that," even "but," are all relevant senses of "*ki*" here, and mutually supporting struts in the bridge, emotional and intellectual, from one major point to another.

The strength of this one broad word, "*ki*," serves well to set the entirety of one long emphasis (27) against the entirety of another (28). Job has worked his way mightily from prolonged righteous indignation in Chapter 27 to prolonged praise of wisdom in Chapter 28. The abrupt dynamic by which he does so is only one of the tempos that the parallelism serves. At other times the emotional adaptiveness moves in a fluidity that makes the transition from an element to its parallel doublet even more striking.

The underlying idea of the whole book can be set in the form of a giant parallelism, which can be seen surfacing in such long homogeneous statements as 27 (the wicked/suffer) and 28 (the wise/see infinitely far):

A	B
the wicked	deserve suffering
A	B (or non-A)
the righteous	suffer
A^1	A
the suffering man	is righteous

The perplexity arising from this series can be resolved only intellectually by the very conclusion of Chapter 28:

> . . . The fear of the Lord, that *is* wisdom;
> And to depart from evil *is* understanding. (28.28)

Job does not abide with this definition, because he craves, and therefore will earn through desire, an emotional and spiritual resolution that God finally provides.

Rhetorical questions throughout, in this chapter or in God's answer from the whirlwind, both evidence the spiritual evocation and extend the parallelism:

> *Art* thou the first man *that* was born?
> Or wast thou made before the hills?
> Hast thou heard the secret of God?
> And dost thou restrain wisdom to thyself? (15.7-8)
> *Are* the consolations of God small with thee?
> Is there any secret thing with thee? (15.11)

Eliphaz himself utters these questions, as rhetorical ones. The parallelism brings them past him. Incidentally they are ambiguous (to be answered either yes or no either immediately or finally). In the force of their assertiveness they tend energetically in the direction of Job's own rhetorical questions about "wisdom," and God's still later ones about His creation before "the first man was born" and the hills made.

Parallelism opens the question up, subsuming them under the giant antithetical parallelism: "the righteous suffer."

And since ideas parallel ideas throughout, with or without an intermediate step or two, a convergence toward unanimity of idea and identity of person, under the most trying spiritual circumstances, is envisioned by the dramatic movement of the whole. In all their affirmations, Job parallels the friends, Job parallels God, the friends parallel each other. The friends, too, parallel God, in whose ritual they begin, and in obeisance to whom they also end.

WORD AND IMAGE

Job and his friends, out in the open air and at some distance from human dwelling, speak amid the splendors and wonders of the natural creation. To the splendor of this creation every single item adduced testifies, at the same time that it enters the multiple correlations of parallelism. In the emerging utterance of his final submission to God, Job does not so much retract what he has said as characterize it for being too limited:

> I know that thou canst do every *thing*
> And *that* no thought can be withholden from thee.
> Who *is* he that hideth counsel without knowledge?
> Therefore have I uttered that I understood not,
> Things too wonderful for me, which I knew not. (42.2-3)

The "things too wonderful for me," the "prodigies" (*niphla'oth*) he says he has himself "uttered." Yet he twice says he cannot know or understand them. They encompass in their reference, by staircase parallelism, not only the "every thing" (*khol,* "all," 42.2) and the "thought" or purpose (*mezimmah,* intent) that cannot be "withholden" from God, but also the majesties of a creation whose visible splendor and terror has just been evoked to bring home Job's limits to himself. The same verb root had been used before by Job of God, "and again thou shewest thyself marvelous upon me" (10.16). Job has, indeed, taken the term over from Eliphaz, "wonders without number," (5.9 equals 9.10). And Elihu employs it twice successively toward the end of his long injunction to Job, "God thundereth marvelously [literally "marvels," *niphla'oth*] with his voice," 37.5; "stand still, and consider the wondrous works [*niphle'oth*] of God," 37.14.

The wonders of man are as nothing by implied comparison. Even the very beasts, over whom the order of Genesis gives man dominion, surpass him when they are seen; they are superior instances of the Creator's inscrutable power. It is through man's knowledge that:

> Iron is taken out of the earth,
> And brass *is* molten *out of* the stone. (28.2)

Zophar puts the same pair into hostile use against the wicked:

> He shall flee from the iron weapon,
> *And* the bow of steel [*neḥushah,* "brass"] shall strike him through.
> (20.24)

And yet man's defensive use of these metals will not prevail over Behemoth, who internalizes their equal in the God-given structure of his body:

> His bones *are as* strong pieces of brass;
> His bones *are* like bars of iron. (40.18)

And, higher in the ascending series of marvels, Leviathan stands so invincible that weapons of these metals are as nothing to him:

> He esteemeth iron as straw,
> *And* brass as rotten wood. (41.27)

It was Job, again, who had introduced the first paralleling of such terms, speaking of himself:

> *Is* my strength the strength of stones?
> Or *is* my flesh of brass? (6.12)

God's majesty is to be read equally in his scrutiny of man's inner intent (*mezimmah* 42.2; *zamam*, devise) and in his deployment through the universe of those beasts among whom even the plain ones attest to the prodigy of his providing for them. Job can always make a sudden transition to the inner and outer marvels of the divine, and so he can bring his humility into implied harmony with an unfathomable purpose. The transition, if sudden, is still felt as a natural step. Job proceeds effortlessly from:

> And brass *is* molten *out of* the stone. (28.2b)

to:

> He setteth an end to darkness . . . (28.3a)

At the same time, though, he is managing with all of his effort. A superelliptical movement of speech may be felt as reaching out at all times to the fullness of creation.

In Job, everything under God's active creation ("I know that thou canst do every *thing*," 42.2) comes into equivalence by virtue of its responsive dependence on the divine agent. Eliphaz slips easily from natural fertility to moral signification, after saying in his first speech that God creates:

> Marvelous things [niphla'ot] without number:
> Who giveth rain upon the earth,

And sendeth waters upon the fields:
To set up on high those that be low; (5.9b-11a)

The animal creation, even those that inspire terror, are asserted by God to be continuous with the human:

Behold now behemoth,
Which I made with thee; (40.15a)

In speaking so, God at once chastens Job by humbling him before the physical terror, and widens his view ("behold") by extending it throughout creation. At the same time, God redirects the mood of a man who has already asserted, in a limited and despairing emphasis, his kinship with animals that lurk, and with those that waken only in darkness:

I am a brother to dragons,
And a companion to owls. (30.29)

Gradually revealed are all the stupendous implications of the continuity between man and "beast," and the link between man and inanimate creation ("stone") which Eliphaz's first speech has already culminated by asserting:

Neither shalt thou be afraid of the beasts of the earth.
For thou shalt be in league with the stones of the field:
And the beasts of the field shall be at peace with thee. (5.22b-23)

The word here for "league," *bherith* ("covenant") is used elsewhere for the tie between man and God,[19] and the verb "be at peace" stands in the causative form. Peace is a prelude to freedom from the fear that God provisionally works to its utmost so that Job may move beyond all of it.

Never are the animals, then, seen simply as static verbal images. Like everything else mentioned in Job, they are swept up in the dynamisms of his situation. Job calls himself a brother to dragons and companion to owls because his disease has transmogrified him, as he says in the very next verse:

My skin is black upon me,
And my bones are burned with heat. (30.30)

He picks up Eliphaz' opening suggestion of fear about animals (4.9-14; 5.22), and compares himself to them in an open rhetorical question:

> The terrors of God do set themselves in array against me.
> Doth the wild ass bray when he hath grass?
> Or loweth the ox over his fodder? (6.4b-5)

Here Job reaches out to the creation which, in our own later schematization, is "lower." Thereby he anticipates God's crescendo of rhetorical questions about beasts. He justifies himself by extending his complaint to adduce a natural, and physical, cause for his outcry: the unfed, men, and the wild ass or the tame ox alike, make their characteristic noises. Yet he also implies a difference between them and himself. These animals are fed in the natural order of things, whether wild or tame, while for himself no "food" can be conceived until God answers him (even though "bread" in 28.5 characteristically "cometh out" of the "earth"). Likenesses and differences also merge in God's descriptions of the animals, whose functions, as they might in a unified creation, parallel man's at several points of resemblance:

> Knowest thou the time when the wild goats of the rock bring forth?
> *Or* canst thou mark when the hinds do calve?
> Canst thou number the months *that* they fulfill?
> Or knowest thou the time when they bring forth?
> They bow themselves, they bring forth their young ones,
> They cast out their sorrows.
> Their young ones are in good liking, they grow up with corn;
> They go forth, and return not unto them.
> Who hath sent out the wild ass free?
> Or who hath loosed the bands of the wild ass?
> Whose house I have made the wilderness,
> And the barren land his dwellings.
> He scorneth the multitude of the city,
> Neither regardeth he the crying of the driver.
> The range of the mountains *is* his pasture,
> And he searcheth after every green thing.
> Will the unicorn be willing to serve thee,

Or abide by thy crib?
Canst thou bind the unicorn with his band in the furrow?
Or will he harrow the valleys after thee?
Wilt thou trust him, because his strength *is* great?
Or wilt thou leave thy labour to him?
Wilt thou believe him, that he will bring home thy seed,
And gather *it into* thy barn?
Gavest thou the goodly wings unto the peacocks?
Or wings and feathers unto the ostrich?
Which leaveth her eggs in the earth,
And warmeth them in dust,
And forgetteth that the foot may crush them,
Or that the wild beast may break them.
She is hardened against her young ones, as though *they were* not hers:
Her labour is in vain without fear;
Because God hath deprived her of wisdom,
Neither hath he imparted to her understanding.
What time she lifteth up herself on high,
She scorneth the horse and his rider.
Hast thou given the horse strength?
Hast thou clothed his neck with thunder?
Canst thou make him afraid as a grasshopper?
The glory of his nostrils *is* terrible. (39.1-20)

The sequence here moves effortlessly from points of resemblance between man and beast, like bearing children and possessing a life span, to points of likeness-in-opposition: "house—the wilderness," unreturning children, improvidence about eggs, fearlessness in battle. Man's typology of the animals is common in the Old Testament and in the Near East generally. Wild goats are traditionally shy, and inaccessibly remote in their wilderness; hinds also are shy, and clean. The "unicorn" (buffalo) is an emblem of fierceness in Assyrian sculpture, typically dangerous and ferocious. The ostrich is here named for its shouting cry (*renanim*), "delighting" in the wilderness and ignoring its offspring, both in sharp contrast to man. The horses are the very sign of the powerfully controlled strength a king can rely on when he owns them.

Here, though, a calmly ordered typology is energetically subverted as the sequence darts back and forth from wild animal to tame, and from tame to wild (lion, raven, wild goat, hind, wild ass, "unicorn," peacock, ostrich, horse, hawk).

The horse transcends the category tame/wild, since it is a serviceable animal of powers too great to be wholly subdued. After Job's first answering statement of insignificance and speechlessness (40.3-5), God expands on animals so ultimately wild that this very category seems insignificant. ("Behold now behemoth . . . etc., 40.15, 41.34.) And God's last words attribute to Leviathan qualities of dominion which Job himself has been revealed as lacking, "He *is* a king over all the children of pride." (41.34)

The emotional response to the animals, as their wonder increases, has come to verge on a response to the divine itself. Since the acts of the animals, through long-range parallelism, repeat themes of the whole (womb, thunder, rock, etc.), Job can the more readily bring his responses to a confrontation of that Creator whose visible presence his resilient outcries have evoked. What he has known all along has been brought to life in the progression of his feelings:

> But ask now the beasts, and they shall teach thee;
> And the fowls of the air, and they shall tell thee:
> Or speak to the earth, and it shall teach thee,
> And the fishes of the sea shall declare unto thee.
> Who knoweth not in all these
> That the hand for the Lord hath wrought this? (12.7-9)

The beasts, as God enumerates and describes them, come into close range and vividly animate Job's attention, leading him into the transcendent perception of the Creator whom he has been stirring and evoking by his persistence. So the beasts, through their function in the dramatic poem, are given authentic, if mysterious, connection with the life of man.

A concentrated force resides in the individual words of the poem. And at the same time, the terms are often notably varied. To begin with, the plethora of divine names used in Job is remarkable for variety and abundance.[20] These names, in their variety, serve as parallels for different aspects of the infinite divine nature. Compared with that, there is a sameness (between man and beast) underlying the infinity ("without number"—5.9, 9.10) of His actual creations. Man has the special covenant with God to which his "covenant" (5.23) with the rest of creation attests. In rising to a conception of the divine mystery, Job negatively stresses the mortality of man; and yet, while doing so, he comes close to propounding an analogy between natural processes in inanimate nature and a man's life after death:

> Drought and heat consume the snow waters:
> *So doth* the grave *those which* have sinned. (24.19)

The peroration of Job's longest speech concludes by bringing up the natural processes once again, with the demand that the cyclic agricultural process reflect his moral bearing:

> If my land cry against me,
> Or that the furrows likewise thereof complain;
> If I have eaten the fruits thereof without money,
> Or have caused the owners thereof to lose their life:
> Let thistles grow instead of wheat,
> And cockle instead of barley.
> The words of Job are ended. (31.38-40)

Job is encompassed by God's creation, as God asserts. Job, then, so long as he remains alive and hopeful, cannot help approaching the Creator of unifying parallels among whatever aspects of creation he might be impelled to name. The parallelism of the verse provides a single principle at once for unity and for diversity among things named. The fact that a statement gets doubled, and more than doubled, in the extensive associativeness of the verse form, brings what anyone says—each of his terms—into a singleness of vision (Job often speaks of God; he is always speaking of God: he dwells on the beasts; the beasts are always evidences of God's creation). At the same time, the fact that the doubling of the verse varies expression easily produces a diversity of terms (there are six names for God;

there are five words for the lion in the short space of two verses: 4.10-11).

The individual words, unstable in tendency, are characteristically condensed in their single occurrences:

But now *they that are* younger than I have me in derision (30.1a)

"They that are younger," *tse'irim,* is a single word that signifies "mean" as well as "young." The double sense works intensely at this moment, both on the side of meanness ("For want and famine *they were* solitary," 30.3a), and on the side of a youth unlike that of Job's dead children ("*They were* children of fools, yea, children of base men," 30.8a). Still, as it happens, Job's description of his own destitution at the end of this chapter ("I am a brother to dragons. ... My skin is black upon me," 30.29-30) will exceed his confrontation of the "mean/young."

The verse jerks powerfully into its intense moments, and out of them freely: this high condensation of vivid utterance, combined with a high fluidity in associateness, gives the poetry of Job a force not attributable to dense words or sweeping strophes alone. Many elements recur in the network of the parallelisms, and yet certain words themselves recur more often than their general Biblical frequency would dictate. Consequently, the stock of elements is less than the stock of words, while at the same time an individual word may get several elements reflected in its single self. This double process (more words than things; more than one thing in a given word) serves to exponentialize a given declaration. As Azariah di Rossi said,[21] in Biblical poetry we should count things rather than words. The abundance of the words (parallelism says everything twice) endows things with an air of comparable abundance; and, as is normal in poetry, the intense economy of the words loads things with significance.

The poetry breaks out constantly in expressions of exact particularity and vividness. "The sparks fly upward," and the desert background is sown with campfires. "My days are swifter than a weaver's shuttle"—the metaphor itself has density beyond the initial comparison. There are the "roots of the sea." The earth contains gold, silver, and precious stones; it is rained on out of the "treasures of the snow," cultivated for its many plants, roamed over by the owl and the unicorn, the wild ox and the ass, the horse and the ostrich, Behemoth and Leviathan.

Mining is seldom mentioned in the Bible, and definitely only in one other place, Deuteronomy 8.9, according to Driver.[22] All the more impressive, for its rarity, is the network of specific activities called up by the single verse (I quote Driver's translation):

> Surely there is a mine for silver,
> And a place for gold which they wash out (28.1)

where both the mine shafts, and a complex refining process in them, are succinctly depicted.

"Roots of the sea" (*shorshe hayyam*, 36.30), in the density of Job, cannot simply be classified as a metaphor. "Root" appears there in a repertoire of uses ranging from the plainly metaphoric "the root of the thing is found in me" (19.28) to plainly literal "Who cut up mallows by the bushes/And juniper roots *for* their meat" (30.4). The word, again through parallelism, serves as a point of recurrent visual intensity, whether metaphoric or not, "My root *was* spread out by the waters" (29.19), "His roots shall be dried up beneath" (18.16), "His roots are wrapped about the heap" (8.17), "He overturneth the mountains by the roots" (28.9), "Thou settest a print upon the heels [literally "roots"] of my feet" (13.27). The word appears also with the force of a verb, "I have seen the foolish taking root" (5.3a), "yea, let my offspring be rooted out" (31.8), "For it *is* a fire *that* consumeth to destruction, and would root out all mine increase" (31.12). The verb is stronger for its rarity; these account for a third of its uses in the entire Old Testament.

The nonmetaphoric objects, in the vividness of their existential independence, outnumber the similes. In their preponderance, they invest the similes and metaphors with their parallels of radiant concretization. "*Ruah,*" spirit, originally and often means wind, and always conveys some sense of a breathing power. "Bone" almost always designates a physical object, but at one point it stands for an inner reality, "One dieth in his full strength" (21.23), literally "in the bone of his completeness," where "completeness" is the same word attributed as "integrity" to Job in 1.1, and "bone" is an idiom for "reality," according to Driver.[23]

Long-range parallelism may concentrate the emphasis of each term, as in

> The firstborn of death shall devour his strength, (18.13)

where "firstborn" and "death," here newly combined, parallel notions that have been repeatedly adduced through the book.

The paralleling motifs intensify the transmutating interchanges of the drama. When Job introduces the womb and the tomb in his very first statement, it is not to compare them but to unify them:

> Naked came I out of my mother's womb,
> And naked shall I return thither:
> The Lord gave, and the Lord hath taken away;
> Blessed be the name of the Lord. (1.21)

He means what he says, and utters for the time being all he has to say, in a verse that parallels a conspectus of his life (21a) with an act of worship (21b). The force of events will give him more to say, but all that he ever says can be expanded from (and as a parallel to) this initial statement, even formally, as always, by virtue of the parallelism and its extensions.

The nakedness, the womb, the coming out of it, are actual. The second nakedness, and the returning thither (*shammah*), only problematically figure an identification between the womb and the interior of the earth. They do not therefore establish a metaphor that can be given a structure and a consequent interpretation. The vagueness leaves a shadow that itself will take on some shape as Job comes to speak further of the interior of the earth, with or without a reference to the place where the body is interred.

As for the "womb" (*beṭen*), it re-enters his thinking again and again, and characteristically with too powerful a dominance to serve merely as a figure of speech. The second verse of this first chapter had spoken of birth, "There were born unto him . . ." And the speech in which Job initiates the dialogue with his long-silent friends brings his birth into relation with the recurrent motif of light and darkness:

> Let the day perish wherein I was born
> And the night *in which* it was said,
> There is a man child conceived. (3.3)

The pressure of dwelling on this thought brings him to the wish that the real light become a real darkness. This thought brings him associatively to a stronger wish: that he had never been born at all.

> Let the stars of the twilight thereof be dark;
> Let it look for light, but *have* none;
> Neither let it see the dawning of the day:
> Because it shut not up the doors of my *mother's* womb [*bhiṭni*],
> Nor hid sorrow from mine eyes.
> Why died I not from the womb? [*reḥem*]
> *Why* did I *not* give up the ghost when I came out of the belly?
> [*mi beṭen yats'athi*, the same phrase as in 1.21] (3.9-11)

Womb and tomb remain as elements to be paralleled through the poem. They are inverted, elaborated on, and realigned. As always, the alteration of a term reveals an alteration of thought and emotion, while its recurrence provides the continuity that the speeches of God will exalt. Of behemoth God begins by almost echoing Job's first words of himself:

> Lo now, his strength *is* in his loins,
> And his force *is* in the navel of his belly. (40.16)

As above, the word once more rendered "belly" is the same one (*bhiṭno*) that is often rendered "womb." In His own first speech He had spoken of the whole sea as coming out of the womb (*reḥem*), again using, as Job does in both the speeches above, the common verb *yatsa'*—and without giving his expression the form of a simile (into which the King James translator renders it, as the italics indicate):

> Or *who* shut up the sea with doors,
> When it brake forth, *as if* it had issued out of the womb? (38.8)

And again:

> Out of whose womb came the ice? (38.29).

The same noun (*beṭen*) is once more linked with the same verb (*yatsa'*), and solidly frozen fresh water replaces flowing salt, without either ice or womb being a metaphor. The answer to this rhetorical question vanishes in the vaunted human ignorance (at the time of the book, which is our time while reading it) about where the ice is formed.

Elihu, too, picks up Job's expressions to re-echo them by locating a spirit or wind (*ruaḥ*) in his own "womb" or vitals, and the range of references in *beṭen*, once more, forbids our taking Elihu's term for a metaphor which would make him explicitly female to the inspiriting God who later answers out of the whirlwind. Elihu:

> For I am full of matter;
> The spirit within me constraineth me.
> *Hetsiqathni ruaḥ biṭni* [literally "the spirit of my womb"]
> Behold, my belly [*bhiṭni*] *is* as wine *which* hath no vent; (32.18-19).

Using *beṭen* twice, Elihu has picked up the thought from a recurring emphasis in Job's immediately preceding speech:

> Did not he that made me in the womb [*beṭen*] make him?
> And did not one fashion us in the womb, [*reḥem*]? (31.15)
>
> . . . .
>
> For from my youth he was brought up with me, as *with* a father,
> And I have guided her from my mother's womb; [*beṭen*]? (31.18)

In these summary statements of his concluding speech, Job calmly deploys a term that had earlier the power to excite him (or show his excitement: the two are one). He displays, both in the first question here and in the second causal conclusion, his mastery of a logic that will still prove inadequate before the Almighty, though he has got beyond the persistent despair of his earlier repetition:

> I should have been as though I had not been;
> I should have been carried from the womb [*beṭen*] to the grave.
> (10.19)

But his speeches can at any time stir into a creative transmutation of this idea, and he anticipates Elihu's use of *beṭen* as well as of *ruaḥ* (*ruaḥ biṭni,* breath-spirit of my vitals, 32.19) by locating his vitals in his living experience:

> My breath [*ruḥi*] is strange to my wife,
> Though I entreated for the children's *sake* of mine own body [*bhitni*]
> (19.17)

The sufferer, plagued by his own sickness, can never get far from his own body, his interior, his *beṭen.* He contemplates what lies in the vitals that are "consumed within me."

> And *though* after my skin *worms* destroy this *body,*
> Yet in my flesh shall I see God:
> Whom I shall see for myself,
> And mine eyes shall behold, and not another;
> *Though* my reins be consumed within me. (19.26-28)

The word for "reins," *ḥeq,* is more general than the translator's term. *Ḥeq,* indicating the vitals of the speaker, parallels the "womb" motif. It echoes all other references to the interiority of a person, and to the interior of the earth.

The paralleling iteration of "womb" keeps bringing the speaker back to the deep interiority of human feeling. Zophar describes the suffering of man, objectified into a third person, by internalizing it inside him, "his meat in his bowels is turned" (20.14), "God shall cast them out of his belly" (*biṭno,* 20.15), "Surely he shall not feel quietness in his belly" (*bhiṭno,* 20.20), "*When* he is about to fill his belly [*bhiṭno*], God shall cast the fury of his wrath upon him" (20.23).

This last statement presents an effect. And of the cause, Eliphaz, too, has said, "They conceived mischief and bring forth vanity,/And their belly [*bhiṭnam*] prepareth deceit" (15.35), rendering an action as a process of giving birth from within. Moreover, repetition of *beṭen* cannot be assigned to the general frequency of the word; about a fourth of all the appearances of *beṭen* in the Old Testament occur in Job.

In parallelism's double statement one item gets partly identified with another and then another. The womb motif (1) is linked to the light motif (2) as well as to the tomb motif (3) in Job's first statement, "Let the day (2) perish (3) in which I was born (1)," especially as he continues to dwell on light and darkness. And light is linked back to the body by the later expression "eyes of flesh" (10.4). The interior of the earth is linked to the interior of the body, the womb with the grave. The treasure to be found in the earth, by comparison, may even first be linked with the idea of death:

> Wherefore is light given to him that is in misery,
> And life unto the bitter *in* soul;
> Which long for death, but it *cometh* not;
> And dig for it more than for hid treasures; (3.20-21)

Here, and throughout Chapter 28 (and elsewhere), there is also, in the multiple dimensions of a paralleling motif, an identification between interiority (of earth or body) and darkness, an identification only implied here, but one strong enough to break out into another motif of dominant opposition between light and darkness, as here at the outset in Chapter 3; in Chapter 28 also; in God's big questions about the origins of heavenly lights; and elsewhere. Light and dark are images too common, of course, to be remarkable, were it not for their unusual connections and applications here. At a certain pitch, as the womb tends to resemble its opposite the tomb, so light is wrought into a darkness: In God's hands, as Eliphaz puts it, the "wise"

> . . . meet with darkness in the daytime,
> And grope in the noonday as in the night. (5.14)

But, later, God brings the darkness (*tsalmaveth*) to light. (12.22) This identification Job expresses still more powerfully later:

> *And* of the shadow of death, without any order,
> And *where* the light *is* as darkness. (10.22b)

This refers to the utter darkness (*tsalmaveth*) "the shadow of death" in the place after death. So that the unity of opposites (light with darkness) subserves the transition from one motif to another (*womb to grave* of 10.19 into *light-darkness*).

Compounded with this excess of identification is the intense particularity of different names for darkness in this passage. *Ḥoshek, 'ephathah, 'ophel,* and *tsalmaveth* occur in just two verses (10.21-2), and the last two are given twice. This "fragmentation" of a motif into several names exemplifies the tendency of Job to emphasize a particularity by varying its nomenclature: the five names for lion in 4.10-11, the many "golds" in 28.15-18, and the multiplicity of names throughout for God, and also for man (*'adam, gever, 'enosh, 'ish, methim*).

The death-perspective even on darkness is contradicted, as well as paralleled, in the course of Elihu's admonitions:

> For his eyes *are* upon the ways of man,
> And he seeth all his goings.
> *There is* no darkness, nor shadow of death, [*tsalmaveth*]
> Where the workers of iniquity may hide themselves. (34.21-2)

And as always the motifs abound. Here "eyes"—"seeth," "ways"—"going," and "iniquity"—"hide" can all be found in paralleled transmutation elsewhere throughout Job.

Matching the proliferation, and paralleled interconnection, of concrete motifs is a set of central prototheological abstractions whose use gives the text its firm scriptural base of affirmation. The multiplicity of these abstractions keeps them from the limitation of exclusive definition. There is, to begin with, *ḥokhmah*, wisdom, the crucial trait of the upright (*yashar*) or righteous (*tsadiq*) man, and the dominant concern of the "Wisdom" books with which Job is traditionally classified. And, independently of given abstract terms, the very form of an utterance may imply sets of abstractions. Job's rhetorical question,

> Hast thou eyes of flesh?
> Or seest thou as man seeth? (10.4)

expects the predominantly negative answer. But the immediately preceding statement, combining the concrete "light-darkness" motif and the abstract "justice-wickedness" motif, offers the contravening positive possibility that essentially God's light is ours—except in those cases of infinite perplexity that Job, as here, perpetually raises:

> *Is it* good unto thee that thou shouldest oppress,
> That thou shouldest despise the work of thine hands,
> And shine upon the counsel of the wicked? (10.3)

Underneath the second of these lines, as throughout the book (often more explicitly) lies a reminiscence of the first creation in Genesis.[24] Here that primary act becomes a question, one that has the effect of keeping the infinitely disparate, man and God, in an unmeasurable union of perception. The word "flesh" comes up again, with another reference to the Creation, and very soon:

> Thou hast clothed me with skin and flesh, (10.11)
> [*'or u bhasar talbisheni*]

Eliphaz, in his first speech, speaking of human capabilities generally, claims that those who "dwell in houses of clay," "die even without wisdom." (4.21, *yamuthu ve l'o bhe ḥokhmah*, "they [shall] die, and not in wisdom.") The imperfect, though used here aphoristically, retains its hint both of provisionality and of some reference to a future. Eliphaz shortly attributes the word, *wise*, to men, but only to subvert it in the direction of the same negative sense:

> He taketh the wise in their own craftiness: (5:13a)

And yet, in the gathering force of dramatic rejoinder, Eliphaz's very negatives imply denigration of a quality that will emerge for triumphant and fairly prolonged, praise, in a distant parallelism to Job's long eulogy of *ḥ'okhmah* (28). Still, Job's antithetical utterance does not leave entirely behind it the uncertainty and limitation of Eliphaz's assertion:

> Whence then cometh wisdom?
> And where *is* the place of understanding? (28.20)

Job has himself been describing wisdom by a comparison that takes a negative form; it is more inaccessible than hidden treasure:

> The depth saith, It *is* not in me:
> And the sea saith, *It is* not with me. (28.14)

And the conclusion of this peroration implies limitation:

> And unto man he said,
> Behold, the fear of the Lord, that *is* wisdom
> And to depart from evil *is* understanding. (28.28)

Job has departed from evil, and has "feared God." His adherence to the maxim he proffers has brought him to a tremendous perplexity. The negative side of "fear," predominating less often in the text than the positive side, still always shadows that other abstraction. In the dramatic context the negative sense may be present even here when fear is postulated as identical with wisdom; for Job overemphasizes his assertion, twice, through "behold," (*hen*) and through the demonstrative "that" (*hi'*):

> Behold, the fear of the Lord, that *is* wisdom
> [*hen yir'ath 'adonai hi' ḥokhmah*]

"Fear" itself, like the wisdom with which it is here identified (so one abstraction, in the unity of God's holiness, leads to others), succeeds at centering itself in the speaker's integrity. Thereby he combines perception and piety, religious vision and the religious act of accepting the limits of vision. The very existence of a range in the term "fear", and its dynamic variation of emphasis, reveal Job's mighty attempt to get into a cosmically squared position. So Job has before been striving to get through the mere moralization of brute creation, to a "wisdom" found, through the range of the word, first in his friends as surrogates of society, next in the beasts, in the old (unless the verse be read as a rhetorical question), and finally in God himself:

> No doubt but ye *are* the people,
> And wisdom shall die with you. (12.2)
>
> . . . .
>
> But ask now the beasts, and they shall teach thee;
> And the fowls of the air, and they shall tell thee:
> Or speak to the earth, and it shall teach thee;
> And the fishes of the sea shall declare unto thee.
> Who knoweth not in all these
> That the hand of the Lord hath wrought this?
> In whose hand *is* the soul of every living thing,
> And the breath of all mankind.
> Doth not the ear try words?
> And the mouth taste his meat?
> With the ancient *is* wisdom;
> And in length of days understanding.
> With him *is* wisdom and strength,
> He hath counsel and understanding. (12.7-13)

Job's integrity allows him the rapid identifications of the final abstractions here. But the comparably unitary assertion of Elihu will reverse his third assertion and make "the ancient" no criterion at all: youth, normally silent, may speak—just as affliction, normally downcast, has been doing all along:

> I *am* young and ye *are* very old;
> Wherefore I was afraid, and durst now show you mine opinion.
> I said, Days should speak,
> And multitude of years should teach wisdom.
> But *there is* a spirit in man:
> And the inspiration of the Almighty giveth them understanding.

LIBRARY ST. MARY'S COLLEGE

Great men are not *always* wise:
Neither do the aged understand judgment. (32.6-9)

Elihu, too, easily combines abstractions here. In his speech Job lacks not perception so much as a fully sounded emotional bearing, a "fear," that Elihu does manifest in his conclusion. And that word, like the others, keeps wavering through its range of meanings. In Job's second speech, the verb is used with the simple meaning "be afraid.":

Ye see *my* casting down ["terror," Driver], and are afraid.
[*tir'u ḥathath va tira'u*] (6.21b)

"Fear" is punned in the Hebrew with "see," suggesting the identification with wisdom that appears more fully elsewhere. The coupling comes up again, twice, in a few verses, where "see" is stronger, but "fear" the same:

Then thou scarest me with dreams
And terrifiest me through visions: (7.14)

Job has just used the word in the full sense, but negatively, when he asserts

To him that is afflicted pity *should be showed* from his friend;
But he forsaketh the fear of the Almighty.
[He that withholdeth kindness from his friend
Forsaketh the fear of the Almighty. Driver] (6.14)

All this has been in answer to the preceding speech of Eliphaz, who uses the verb in the extreme of its minimum sense:

Thou shalt be hid from the scourge of the tongue:
Neither shalt thou be afraid of destruction when it cometh.
At destruction and famine thou shalt laugh:
Neither shalt thou be afraid of the beasts of the earth.
(5.21-22)

The repetitions of Eliphaz' prophecy will come true only after the condition has come about that these very prophetic words will help to bring about. True fear dwells with God, Bildad comes later to say:

Dominion and fear *are* with him. (25.2a)

This time, though, the word for fear is not *yir'ah,* the "normal" term, but one of its more intense and physically shattering variants, *phaḥadh* "terrifying-ness." And this is the mood that God brings upon Job by describing the terrifying monsters among brute creation. The voice from the whirlwind uses other variant words for fear. So, for the horse:

> The glory of his nostrils *is* terrible.
> [the glory of his snorting, terror
> *hod naḥro 'emah*] (39.20b)

Leviathan is alone upon earth as to lack "dismay" (*ḥath,* the same root as *ḥathath,* "casting down," in 6.21b cited above):

> Upon earth there is not his like,
> Who is made without fear. ["dismay"] (41.33)

Yet the full sense of the abstraction lies, through parallelism, always so close at hand, that it may combine and identify easily with others, as in Eliphaz' opening speech about Job's good action:

> *Is* not *this* thy fear, thy confidence,
> Thy hope, and the uprightness of thy ways?
> [Is not thy fear (of God) thy confidence
> (And) thy hope the perfectness of thy ways? Driver] (4.6)

This rapid, easy transition through a string of four terms begins with "fear" and ends with the very word attributed to Job in the first verse:

> . . . and that man was perfect and upright,
> [*tam ve yashar*] (1.1)

The possibilities in the range of a word allow, at their utmost, a contradiction. The contradiction built into the word-atoms parallels the contradiction of the whole, the schematic contradiction of a just man suffering, and the dramatic contradiction of Job's neither wholly acquiescing therein, as the friends urge, nor simply reacting to "Curse God and die," as his wife recommends (2.9). The very word his wife uses, *barak*,[25] embodies such a contradiction, because it means "bless" in its most normal usage, though in its early occurrences in the narrative, Job uses it to suggest that his sons may have "cursed God in their hearts" (1.5). Still, the verb is used in its normal sense when God is said to "bless" Job (1.10), only to be given its opposite sense in the next verse, when Job will "curse thee to thy face (1.11)." But Job uses *barak* in the straight sense when he speaks after his first affliction

> The Lord gave, and the Lord hath taken away;
> Blessed be the name of the Lord. (1.21)

This interchange of oppositions in the single verb *barak* is resolved as a different verb is used, when Job really did "open his mouth and cursed his day" (3.1): the verb now is the new one for the book, but regular one for "curse," *qalal*; "make light," "render contemptible" are meanings of the verb present here, as well as "curse." *Barak* is used again in the straight sense at the very end of the book, linking the epilogue with the prologue, when it is said that God "blessed the latter end of Job" (42.12). The contradictory usage is echoed by being put in a negative and conditional form for Job's closing asseveration, "If his loins have not blessed me." (31.20a) Job has used the word early in the same speech of a dying man's statement about himself:

> The blessing of him that was ready to perish came upon me;
> (29.13a)

Since these are all the uses of *barak* in Job, the preponderance of them keeps in view the word's contradictory senses. Contradiction often gets fixed, too, by setting opposites directly against each other.

> Wilt thou condemn me, that thou mayest be righteous? (40.8b)
> [*tarshi'eni lema'an titsdaq?*]

The root *rasha'*, "evil," is set by God into impossible opposition with a key term which would express Job's traditional piety, or *tsedaqah,* righteousness. An underlying contradiction may qualify even a straight assertive statement of rhetorical question, as in:

> Shall mortal man [*'enosh*] be more just than God?
> Shall a man [*gaver*] be more pure than his Maker? (4.17)

Here, the explicit contradiction of the impossibility that lesser should exceed Greater in the superlative qualities of *tsadak* ("be righteous, just,") and purity, gets underscored in the contradiction between *'enosh,*[26] a word implying that man is weak and frail (as also in 7.1 and 7.17) and *gaver,* which suggests man's heroic strength, the word being used regularly (though seldom so in Job) for a military hero.

Biblical utterance generally possesses an expansible quality that allows a single phrase to stand as the text for numerous sermons, as Job itself is used for the voluminous series of Gregory the Great's *Moralia.* This expansibleness has been turned back inward by the verse of Job. Not only does each verse comment on and condense others. The individual terms, abstract and concrete, change and recombine under the pressure of the dynamic progress of the dramatic voicings. Simple conclusions, of wide implications by themselves, get a further syntactic weighting in such a phrase, formed of only two abstractions, as:

> They were confounded because they had hoped;
> [*boshu khi bhaṭaḥ*] (6.20a)

"Hope" (*bhaṭaḥ* means also "trust") is put in the emphatic pausal position, and means more than any possible word to translate it, especially here.

In such a network of references it would be easy to construct a coherent, though unsystematic, set of anthropological abstraction-relations. The text itself almost does so, breaking out persistently in proverbs which the context renders always as more than the steady, undeniable commonplaces of *Proverbs,* which they resemble (and sometimes perhaps echo): "Proverb" (*mashal*) is a word used in a fuller sense by Job, to mean story, and parable and argument also (27.1, 29.11).

> For wrath killeth the foolish man,
> And envy slayeth the silly one. (5.2)

This is a proverb, and something more. Eliphaz' interacting and expanding terms give this statement a full, positive ring: the abstractions strive to compass something. However, they never really merge with the concretions which also, as we have seen, produce their own interactions and expansions. Eliphaz is not only offering summary wisdom; he is dramatically cutting short the concrete references to light and darkness in Job's preceding speech. The concretions will take over again, though most fully when God has come to the heights of his own final utterance. Eliphaz' brisk, unimaged clarity, in its abstractness, only mimes the piety that Job more fully enacts. In either abstract or concrete form, pious utterance remains constantly subject to the inner energy propelling these verses.

That energy opens, syntactically, into the recurrent, characteristic form of the rhetorical question, so assertive, often, that it can be answered either yes or no, either for the moment or generally:

> Doth God pervert judgment? (8.3)

Obviously no, since he is God (as Bildad here means). Obviously yes, since we have seen from the prologue how he accepts Satan's wager. No, in general, since he is God, but yes in particular, since Job stands before us. Obviously yes in general: his ways are a mystery Job sets forth; and no in particular, since Job is justified in his latter end. The force of Bildad's succinctness, as he puts the question in three loaded Hebrew words; the propulsion of his tirade, as he includes it in a rapid-fire series of four such questions, would act to drown out all these multiple possibilities in a single asseveration so obvious that it can be put fearlessly in a question, *God perverts judgment?* The multiple possibilities, in the dynamic movement of the drama, drown him out in turn, and keep the possibilities interchanging till God's voice comes out of the whirlwind. He keeps the other end open by providing his answers in the form of tremendous rhetorical questions. And these bring Job to respond before the magnificent final parade of creative acts. God states these, too, in the form of queries whose answer is at once obvious and unfathomable, like the central question of the book.

SEQUENCE

The force of the emotions in The Book of Job, its convincing dramatic vitality, carries it on through its expansive set of coruscating utterances. It comes clear in the sum and not in the separate acts. Each person's responses move the thought of the drama on. Each one's reactions, in turn, govern the drama's unstable winding through sets of assumptions that themselves remain stable throughout: Job is a sinful man, Man is feeble and sinful, God made him and is just, God is inscrutable and so man's life is inscrutable; the world is majestic, and so is God; God is swift to act, life passes swiftly, all men are mortal, He should not care to hurt such frail creatures, He should allow them peace in their brief earthly span, man cannot be justified in an encounter with God, a just man has nothing to fear, it is hard to see how God is fair, God should be trusted unto the death, "Though he slay me, yet will I trust in him." The Book of Job does not strike a solution for these several assumptions, or a resolution among them, but rather a profound re-enactment of a human psyche so broad in its responses to God as to render them their wholeness by incorporating them in the dynamic of an overall reaction. Thus Job's existence sustains the human spirit far more than a solution itself could.

The drama, being an internal one, has no stage props other than the desert and the sky, and no set of plotted events other than these deeply foregrounding emotional confluences, dominating in solitary splendor a stage which is only imagined. Georg Fohrer[27] finds Job combined from three prototypes of literary form, the "wisdom contest," the "judicial contest," and the psalm. Yet these forms

LIBRARY ST. MARY'S COLLEGE

constantly undergo blending and distortion, and each takes on the functions of the others under the unifying onrush of a speaker's voice.

If there is an emotional leap from sentence to sentence, and an emotional set in the integrating asseverations of a single speech, then that very associative principle allows greater scope for a leap from speech to speech. Just as what a sentence parallels may be far as well as near, so a speech may respond to one thing, and evoke another, by omitting the parallel topic as well as by repeating it, inverting it, or qualifying it. Consequently, a given speech stands automatically in multiple parallel, just from the schema of the book. Job's second speech parallels his first speech in certain ways, and his third speech; it also parallels what it answers, the first speeches of Eliphaz, Bildad, and Zophar (and also their second speeches, and so on). Furthermore everything said stands in anticipatory parallelism to God's final utterance.

The possibility of association beyond the immediately preceding speech is insisted on, as it were, by the grace note of a still further set to parallel all of these, the long, unbroken speech of the young Elihu.[28] A leap is needed to accommodate his speech in the drama, but there are leaps everywhere, even in the movement from one sentence to another. Moreover, any speech at the outset seems a near impossibility after the seven days' silence, and after the utter weariness of a Job who must speak to give the friends any scope at all.

This resurgent susceptibility of emotion is far from operating chaotically, though its order is an internally expansive one. It is set, to begin with, in a formal framework: the friends have come to mourn ritually the misfortune of a friend who is afflicted as the final, hidden test-case of a divine response to questioning. Job himself is sustained at either end of his life by rituals: of the worship to which he refers, of his acts of atonement for sins his sons may have committed (1.5), even of the prayer-like statements throughout his speeches. The friends' last act for Job is to perform the ritual of ordered sacrifices.

The speeches, too, are set in an order. Job's statement evokes replies, each of which evokes his reply, which evokes a second cycle of three replies in turn, which evoke his further replies, which evoke a third cycle of only two more replies. The missing third speech of the third cycle is abundantly supplied by the superseding cadenza of Elihu's speech, longer than any previous ones, as Job's speeches had tended to be longer than the friends'. But God's culminating speech is still longer, though it is broken by Job's now succinct two verses of atonement (40.4-5).

God's speech and all the others are of course framed into the order of parallel verses, and into all the pregnant logical implications following from parallelism; they have also from time to time—if not steadily—a strophic[29] order. Inside these orders, syntactic, rhythmic, and dramatic, the strong impulsions of emotional reaction gather their groupings of insistences. Once God has afflicted Job's person "with sore boils from the sole of his foot unto his crown," (2.7) he does not "bless the name of the Lord," (1.21) as he had done in response to being stripped of wealth and offspring. Job responds to his pain by seven days of silence. The three friends gathered from afar, by their ritual weeping are responding to his response when they keep a like silence, "and none spake a word unto him: for they saw that *his* grief was very great." (2.13)

Job's second response, as the long, presumably monotonous time settles upon him, is to emit utterances quite different in character, as in statement, from his earlier four lines of submission. Silent suffering makes him prolix. He returns to his earlier conjunction of birth and death:

> Naked came I out of my mother's womb,
> And naked shall I return thither: (1.21a)

But now he intensifies birth and death, in a wish that would so identify them as to nullify them. Job wishes the past would collapse into total nonexistence—*past as well as future*—a condition that only God is capable of producing. (The imagined act indicates, therefore, at the extreme of Job's suffering, an extreme theological understanding of the divine power):

> Let the day perish wherein I was born,
> And the night *in which* it was said,
> There is a man child conceived. (3.3)

He dwells with this thought for seven whole verses, countering at the outset, by this prolixity, his earlier terse aptness.

When he flags from this idea, it is to vary it with a weaker but more compact version of itself, "Why died I not from the womb?" (3.11a), substituting an infant mortality for a nonexistent conception, and letting causal assertion, once he has brought himself into the world of cause, take over from mere extravagant wish. The speech is now made to hinge on a causal particle (*ki*, "for," "therefore, "that") and a simple contrary-to-fact verb:

> For now should I have lain still and been quiet,
> I should have slept: then had I been at rest, (3.13)

The succinct inflection of Hebrew does not permit these verbs, strongly paralleling in four repetitions, to take more than the form of completeness or consecutiveness: they are perfects, while the imperfect comes regularly into such use in Job. The simplicity of these verbs acts as a foreshortening of the conditional element in them (to which no inflectional constituent in Hebrew corresponds —and so they thrust the condition the more nakedly on the syntax-by-context). Resting on the notion that the dead have rest, Job goes on to turn this imagined palliation into an occasion for nascent indignation: why are the rest-less not allowed to die? As he comes to himself in the exemplary third person, he expresses himself curtly, not bothering to repeat his main clause (though the King James translators did, as their italics always indicate):

> *Why is light given* to a man whose way is hid . . . ? (3.23a)

Just touching on this definition of himself, he reverts to enumerating his "sighing," "roarings," and fears, and concludes on a simple narration of what happened: "yet trouble came" (3.26b) [literally "turbulence" or "quaking,": *roghez*, the word used again in 14.1, "Man teems with quaking"].

Eliphaz, first to speak as the eldest, does not pick up any of these threads. Instead he asks about the very fact of Job's speaking at all, beginning with a question:

> *If* we assay to commune with thee, wilt thou be grieved?
> But who can withhold himself from speaking? (4.2)

The question becomes not only the initial but the characteristic opening response of the friends, in six out of eight speeches, as Driver[30] notes. Eliphaz' word "grieved" (*til'eh*) carries with it the implication "wearied"; he is asking whether Job can stand any of what in fact he must hear all. Yet he drops the question to praise Job's former good advice to other sufferers, letting himself slip gradually into a lengthy disquisition on the guilt of sufferers:

> Remember, I pray thee, who *ever* perished, being innocent? (4.7)

And so he has let suspicion take the upper hand, under the pressure of seven days of polite silence. By 4.13 he is giving his words the authority of "visions" (*ḥezyonoth*):

> In thoughts from visions of the night,
> When deep sleep falleth on men. (4.13)

"Visions" is a word with religious overtones, as is the "deep sleep" (*tardemah*), here designated by the same word, a relatively rare one, used for Adam's sleep when Eve was taken out of his side (Genesis 2.21), when God made a promise to Abraham (Genesis 15.12), and when Elihu says God speaks to men generally (33.15). Trying to rouse in Job a fear Job has already expressed, by telling of God's power over five varieties of powerful lion, he speaks of his own terror graphically ("the hair of my flesh stood up" 4.15), and goes on to contrast the man, who is "frail," with God, who is . . . not "strong," but rather "just" and "pure." The gap between frailty and justice—which after all Job is to remark on—is now filled by assertion; as though Eliphaz were becoming uneasy before the main question he has now tacitly brought up.

After touching on the harm that comes to those appurtenances of the foolish man wherein Job has suffered, children and harvest, he passes over any mention of Job's disease to generalize about human trouble and to emphasize what he himself would do (*'ulam 'ani:* "Indeed I") under the circumstances:

> I would seek unto God,
> And unto God would I commit my cause (5.8)

The thought allows him to relieve his mind, and to leave the real Job behind for an imagined Job, in a eulogy of God which culminates in asserting Job's natural harmony with creation:

> For thou shalt be in league with the stones of the field
> And the beasts of the field shall be at peace with thee. (5.23)

and a naturally seasonable death:

> Thou shalt come to *thy* grave in a full age (5.26)

He puts the seal on this seeming unreality (of what actually comes true) by including the friends in a unanimity that pretends intellectual inquiry instead of emotional palliation:

> Lo this, we have searched it, so it *is;*
> Hear it, and know thou *it* for thy good. (5.27)

Eliphaz closes ranks by using the plural "we," and Job takes his cue from that. His response to Eliphaz' evasiveness is to express vividly the actuality of his suffering, a response that rouses him beyond the somewhat passive state of his first speech. He parallels Eliphaz' reference to stones and beasts by mentioning animals (wild ass and ox) and natural phenomena to either side of Eliphaz' "stones of the field," sand and snow. In his concreteness about the world they live in, Job now approximates more closely than Eliphaz had the tenor of God's later speech. Job begins by expostulating against Eliphaz' assertion that "we have searched it" by the counterdemand that his vexed "grief" (*k'as*, "vexation") be really, "thoroughly weighed" (*shaqol yisshaqel*) repeating the verb for emphasis:

> Oh that my grief were thoroughly weighed,
> And my calamity laid in the balances together! (6.2)

He dwells on the weight of his grief in one image, only to be driven to another, and still another.

> For now it would be heavier than the sand of the sea: . . .
> For the arrows of the Almighty *are* within me,
> The poison whereof drinketh up my spirit:
> The terrors of God do set themselves in array against me. (6.3-4)

He counters Eliphaz' request that he appeal to God by saying, for the first time explicitly, how intimately and fully he stands under God's affliction. To name the terrors is to hold out against them: to speak of lacking food ("Doth the wild ass bray when he hath grass" 6.5), or of having a food that is tasteless ("Can that which is unsavoury be eaten without salt?/Or is there *any* taste in the white of an egg?" 6.6) is to demand some other satisfaction than Eliphaz has begun by offering. Job works himself up to a direct accusation:

> My brethren have dealt deceitfully as a brook,
> *And* as the stream of brooks they pass away; (6.15)

Still, he couches the accusation in a language of appeal, by calling them "my brethren," though the third person preserves a distance that Eliphaz had set up. This turns into an address in the second person (6.21-29), as he accuses them not of an intellectual flaw but an emotional one, not of inconsistency but of a fear that renders him null:[31]

> For now ye are nothing;
> Ye see *my* casting down, and are afraid. (6.21)

The pun on "see" and "are afraid" (*tir'u hathath va tira'u*) emphasizes the causal connection between them. Job's disappointment is the greater that, until Eliphaz had spoken, the attentions of his friends might have led him to expect a comfort actually impossible in the heaviness of his affliction, and now proved to be lacking. As Driver[32] says, "He compares his friends picturesquely to a *wàdy*, a stream—such as is common in and about Palestine—running along a rocky valley, which may be turbid and swollen in winter, but completely dry in summer; and his own disappointment to that of a thirsty caravan, journeying hopefully towards such a *wàdy*, only to find its waters dried up through the heat." Heat, indeed, (*ḥamam*) is the root word for the "poison" of the Almighty's arrows (6.4); and the earlier passage further parallels this one because the "poison" "drinketh up" his spirit. He pleads for a more explicit communication of his wrongdoing ("cause me to understand wherein I have erred," 6.24), at the same time claiming that his own discernment is adequate to the task:

> Is there iniquity in my tongue?
> Cannot my taste discern perverse things? (6.30)

The image, again, repeats the earlier one which implicity subverts his assertion; what good will his taste do if he has said that what he gets now is tasteless:

> Can that which is unsavoury be eaten without salt?
> Or is there *any* taste in the white of an egg?
> The things *that* my soul refused to touch
> *Are* as my sorrowful meat. (6.6-7)

He now follows the lead of Eliphaz' emotional drift by reverting to generalities—reverting in so far as the immediate situation is concerned, though his emotions, as distinct from those of Eliphaz, tend elsewhere, in the light of where his sufferings ultimately lead him. For Job, to introduce generalities is to strive to account for the universal context in which what he undergoes may have some meaning. But the generality about man's appointed time on earth (echoing Eliphaz' statement of death in due season) lasts only a verse, and a semi-rhetorical question qualifies it.

From a concrete depiction of his suffering (7.2-7), Job comes back round to his death (7.9-10). But now, in the process he has evoked by speaking so much, his thought evokes not the wish to die but the wish to speak more. He has slipped anyway from the use of the first person into the generality of a third person:

> He shall return no more to his house,
> Neither shall his place know him any more.
> Therefore I will not refrain my mouth;
> I will speak in the anguish of my spirit;
> I will complain in the bitterness of my soul. (7.10-11)

In the subtle direction of Job's feeling from the beginning, God stands always in view as a dynamic possibility; for the friends, by contrast, he is a fixed, and therefore remote, point.

Now Job (7.12-21) speaks right out to God, asking if he himself is one of those monsters of inanimate or animate creation that later God will Himself invoke. Thus, once again, the phrasing in Job's seemingly negative attitude anticipates, by the very boldness of its purview, God's positive resolution:

> *Am* I a sea, or a whale, [*tannin,* sea-monster; possibly Tiamat, the Babylonian world-serpent. Later he will be a "brother" to *tannin,* dragon(s), 30.29]
> That thou settest a watch over me? (7.12)

Instead of repeating his wish to die, he now complains that his fears are such as to make him wish to die, putting the death wish at one remove. At the same time he questions the very existence of man, so much so that he comes abruptly (even if hypothetically) to admit what if taken for other than a momentary lapse of his desperate thrashing would obviate the need for anything other than expiation:

> I have sinned; what shall I do unto thee,
> O thou preserver of men?
> . . . .
> And why dost thou not pardon my transgression,
> And take away mine iniquity? (7.20-21a)

The admission[33] on which Job now closes his second speech is a startling one, conceding all that Eliphaz had wished. So startling is it that Bildad does not even assimilate it as the momentary lapse of dire distress, but, rather, profoundly ignores Job's remarks to continue the first friend's speech, in a blunter vein.

Bildad's honest feeling does catch some of the truth of plain speaking:

> Doth God pervert judgment?
> Or doth the Almighty pervert justice? (8.3)

But he oversimplifies the conditions, and thereby overlooks in his next statement the fact that Job had already performed sacrifices for the possible sins of his children (1.5):

> If thy children have sinned against him,
> And he have cast them away for their transgression; (8.4)

Carried away by the sweep of his own utterance, he characterizes Job by inverting the very terms "upright" (*yashar*; 1.1; 8.6), and "perfect" (*tam*, 1.1; 8.20) which the prose narrative had begun by attributing unequivocally to Job. Bildad puts them in a contrary-to-fact condition:

> If thou *wert* pure and upright;
> Surely now he would awake for thee,
> And make the habitation of thy righteousness prosperous. (8.6)
> . . . .
> Behold, God will not cast away a perfect man, (8.20)

If Bildad's foreshortenings turn out to be prophetic of Job's fate, it will not be in these terms, so preliminary that they deny the very problem. They are so traditional, too, that they lump the "former age" (*dhor*, "generation," where the plural would be expected) into a monolithic and unequivocal stand: "For inquire, I pray thee, of the former age," (8.8). Moreover, Job, himself, from the vantage of The Book of Job, stands in the former time of the patriarchal age a millennium before. The book already harks back, a fact that mutes and qualifies Bildad's harking back.

Bildad's very curtness allows Job the condescension of a mild reply, and it provides the unconscious side-effect of relieving Job by allowing him to remind Bildad of the problem:

> I know *it is* so of a truth:
> But how should man be just with God? (9.2)

Job takes Bildad's abstract noun, justice (*tsedheq*, 8.3), and humanizes it by giving it the dramatic function of a verb (*yitsdaq*, "justify," 9.2).

His momentary superiority imbues Job with the strength to redirect his own, and Bildad's, prior depression over man's insignificance, into an exclamation, emotionally steadying, about the power of God. This time Job draws even closer in phrasing and in mood to God's later words:

> Which alone spreadeth out the heavens,
> And treadeth upon the waves of the sea;
> Which maketh Arcturus, Orion,
> And Pleiades, and the chambers of the south;
> Which doeth great things past finding out;
> Yea, and wonders without number. (9.8-10)

The last verse repeats almost the identical phrasing of Eliphaz' first speech (5.9), but sets it in a context more wrought with response to the scope of God, where Eliphaz had been stressing His dependability. In Job's context of feeling, the actual terms "great things" and "wonders without number" take on an exuberance fuller than Eliphaz' cursory designation: they summarize as well as state. Riding this exuberance, Job states his "justness" or righteousness personally with the same verb he had used impersonally to introduce his speech:

> Whom, though I were righteous [*tsadhaqti*], yet would I not answer,
> *But* I would make supplication to my judge. (9.15)

Job's very pitch of excitation can go either way, and under the constant impact of his physical suffering ("And he breaketh me with a tempest,/And multiplieth my wounds without cause," 9.17), he leads himself into the perplexity of a human being's ever being able to make himself righteous or just ("if I justify [*'etsdaq*] myself, mine own mouth shall condemn me:" 9.20a). His distraction brings him to supplement Bildad's statement "God will not cast away a perfect man," with a corollary emerging from the divine transcendence he has just been praising and deploring:

> *Though* I *were* perfect, *yet* would I not know my own soul:
> I would despise my life.
> This *is* one *thing,* therefore I said *it,*
> He destroyeth the perfect and the wicked. (9.21-22)

Job is now recombining the earlier assumptions and repeating the assertion of universal mortality. But the speech, dominated by a different tonal range, points in a new direction. At the end, though man be unjustifiable, the thought of mimetically purifying himself ("If I wash myself with snow water,/And make my hands never so clean"; 9.30) passes over its despairing consequence that he would be dirtied again ("Yet shalt thou plunge me in the ditch,/And mine own clothes shall abhor me" 9.31), to raise the new possibility of confronting God directly ("Neither is there any daysman betwixt us" 9.33) and without fear:

> *Then* would I speak, and not fear him; (9.35a)

But this condition can only be imagined, not realized:

> But *it is* not so with me. (9.35b)

Job goes on to imagine his address to God, balancing his speech (10.1-20) about equally between afflictions and marvels, justice and inscrutability, till he reverts to a newly conditional version of his old wish for non-existence. Therein he concentrates on iteration about a death now seen as utterly black, but in an indefinite future:

> I should have been as though I had not been;
> I should have been carried from the womb to the grave.
>
> . . . .
>
> Let me alone, that I may take comfort a little,
> Before I go *whence* I shall not return,
>
> . . . .
>
> A land of darkness, as darkness *itself*;

> *And* of the shadow of death, without any order,
> And *where* the light *is* as darkness. (10.19-22)

Job is beginning to master himself by a kind of increasing inclusiveness that makes this speech more energetic in its emotional transitions, as wider in its intellectual range, than the four previous speeches, to all of which it refers. Job has now mustered enough firmness of spirit to base his opening on the very legal abstractions that, while they tend to subvert one another, do diagram his perplexity. Still, his answer to Bildad has got quickly beyond Bildad, to compose a tightness of logical relations phrased less suppositiously than his earlier "death" speech. This speech is therefore more daring as it enters the extremes of good and evil, managing to produce a simple proposition that holds:

> *Though* I *were* perfect, *yet* would I not know my soul:
> [*tam 'ani l'o 'eda' naphshi* (9.21a)]

Five Hebrew words; and their succinctness carries the effect of a summary.

Zophar, however, does not repeat Job's utterance, nor respond to it in his response. Instead, he begins, much as had Bildad, by accusing Job of garrulity, and by oversimplifying his point:

> For thou hast said, My doctrine *is* pure,
> And I am clean in thine eyes. (11.4)

Zophar is now emotionally involved in the dialogue to the extent that he comes at Job's speeches rather than first at his prior behavior, defining his friend's words as a plethora ("multitude," 11.2), as "lies" (11.3), and as mocking God in such a way as to call for rebuke; "When thou mockest, shall no man make thee ashamed?" (11.3). To say this is to take the cue from Bildad and Eliphaz, with whom he stands in the sympathy of similarity. He buttresses his stand by an appeal to human insignificance, as though Job had not already evoked that himself, and by exhorting Job to go through the ritual act of removing wickedness and iniquity when Job had already done so by putting on sackcloth and by making speeches which God will later praise ("spoken of me *the thing which is* right" 42.8).

Zophar, under the protection of being the last speaker in the sequence of friends, enjoys a kind of calmness in conclusion; and he can offer that calmness to Job as an inducement to hope for something other than the utter darkness he himself had concluded by describing:

> And *thine* age shall be clearer than the noonday;
> Thou shalt shine forth, thou shalt be as the morning. (11.17)

Since the three have now closed ranks, Job responds by a sarcasm shot with a resignation recognizably akin to Zophar's calm:

> No doubt but ye *are* the people,
> And wisdom shall die with you. (12.2)

But having got this off his chest, he drops it to try to make them listen to him by insisting on his equality, and on the platitude of what they have been saying:

> I *am* not inferior to you;
> Yea, who knoweth not such things as these? (12.3)

This note of complaint soon gives way to the longest, most comprehensive, and most awestruck recital so far of the Creator's powers (12.7-25). Having begun to point lessons from the creation to his friends ("But ask now the beasts, and they shall teach thee;" 12.7), Job gets carried away in the persistence of his own contemplation. That he dwells on a subject tells us much about the steadiness of his mind, as does his drift into a choice of the subject itself. Still, he cannot release himself from the sway of resentment, and the nagging repetition of his initial words ("I *am* not inferior to you:" 12.3b equals 13.2b) brings him and what he says about God back within the circle of his own plea for self-justification. But the confidence that had been welling up earlier, momentarily suppressed, emerges in a new absolutism of reliance on God. To hold God up in a light that will scold his friends gives Job the impetus to catch a foretaste of his final security:

> Though he slay me, yet will I trust in him:
> But I will maintain mine own ways before him. (13.15)

The spirit of man, as here conceived and expressed, has always accessible to it a fluidity of emotion dynamic enough to rush into total awareness. This statement would be premature, as some maintain,[34] only if the speeches were set in the neat logical relations into which some commentators overschematize them. In the light of his new, if momentary, clarity, Job's demand for the charges against him, and his reassertion of the insignificance of man, have a more optimistic ring than his earlier phrasings of these ideas. To define man now as "teeming with turbulence," (*sheva' roghez*, 14.1) is to exceed the turbulence by standing off from it to name it. He concludes his own speech, and the first cycle of speeches, by declaring emphatically but succinctly the congruence (through the parallelism) of the body's pain and the soul's mourning:

> But his flesh upon him shall have pain,
> And his soul within him shall mourn. (14.22)

Lamentation provides the tonic note, but Eliphaz takes up as though he had not heard it, deferring to Job's sorrow not at all, and to Job's perceptions only by opening the possibility that Job's speech may prove him "wise" enough now to lapse into silence—as the patness of Job's conclusion above, and even its being put in the third person, might portend;

> Should a wise man utter vain knowledge,
> And fill his belly with the east wind? (15.2)

Eliphaz proves himself to persist in a feeling closer to his earlier speeches. He is more set in his ways than the more heavily afflicted Job. At this point Job has run a gamut in four speeches. Now that the leading friend has been the first to utter a second speech, Eliphaz' obsessiveness, through his own long silence during the other five speeches, reveals that his greater freedom, as the one to start, only permits him a greater complacency.

Setting the wise man over against Job draws Eliphaz into depicting man as unclean (15.14-17), and then into exaggerating the wicked man (15.20-35) with a fervor that faintly veils in generality the application to Job he could not here explicitly claim. For Job by no stretch of the imagination could have acted as proudly and unjustly as the man of whom Eliphaz speaks, though in his next and last speech Eliphaz will break into explicit, unfair accusation of his friend (22.6-11). At the moment a certain balance between "wise" and "evil" obtains over Eliphaz' utterance, a balance already tipping into ungrounded expostulation against evil men toward the end. Eliphaz finishes by condemning the sinner who combines hypocrisy and pride (*ḥaneph* implies both):

> For the congregation of hypocrites (*haneph*) shall be desolate
> . . . .
> They conceive mischief, and bring forth vanity,
> And their belly prepareth deceit. (15.34-5)

The sensitive Job does not miss the hint about his own speeches reiterated in the last verse, and he retorts by formulating an inference about the friends' hardheartedness that Eliphaz' failure to get beyond the first round of speeches has now justified:

> Miserable comforters *are* ye all. (16.2b)
> [literally "comforters of trouble," *'amal*, the same word Eliphaz had used in his first speech, "Man is born unto trouble, as the sparks fly upward," 5.7]

Eliphaz' obfuscation-by-exaggeration cannot have been other than willful, and to avoid the question of the "trouble" is to want to perpetuate it. Job now imagines what he would do if he were in their position toward a suffering friend (16.4-6), but the thought does not release him. His very position subjects him under quickening response to whatever they may say, and the effect of their evading accusations has been to drive him deeper into his depression, which now dominates all the rest of his speech.

Now it is not the eyes of widows that will fail, but the eyes of children (17.5)—the children of [the one] "that speaketh flattery to *his* friends," the evil man whom the friends' accusations make Job out to be, when the fact of accusing him shows them to be that themselves. Because of the false friends, Job has become "a byword of the people" (*mashal,* also "tale," "proverb"), and his own eye "is dim by reason of sorrow," (17.7) (*k'as,* the "vexation" that Eliphaz asserted in his first speech "killeth the foolish man," 5.2). As for hypocrites, the "innocent shall stir up himself" against them (17.8). Job strives to turn the tables on the friends, making them hypocritical in their accusation of hypocrisy. His effort does not alleviate his feelings, and he runs down, as he had earlier, on conjuring forth the physical corruption of the grave. Expression of his emotion has regressed to the unrelieved lamentation of his initial obsession with death, and with himself, to the exclusion of either the friends or God.

Bildad responds to this speech in the pattern nearly as familiar by now as the formulaic opening words, "Then answered Bildad." After berating Job for garrulity, he ignores the main burden of what Job has said and twists some of the details. Where Job has said that God "tore" him, using a verb (*taraph*) applied to beasts of prey (16.9), Bildad inverts the proper sensitiveness to make the friends touchy instead of Job, and asks "wherefore are we counted as beasts?" (18.3), going on to declare it is Job who is the wild beast to himself: "He teareth himself in his anger" (or "thou that tearest").

The platitudes about the darkness of the wicked have long since demonstrated their inefficacy at succoring Job, or even leading him to contrition. Bildad's main purpose therefore emerges as the assertion of his own righteousness, which he emphasizes by avoiding all the interactions of range in Job's speeches, or even Eliphaz', to stay on a single topic: the afflictions of the wicked. These are highlighted by the recurrent figures of the trap, the oncoming darkness, and the destroyed tent.

Since the friends have given him nothing further he can address himself to, Job is thrown back on immersing himself in his own reactions, a course that is bound to break him. And it does bring him to the dramatic crescendo of crying out for pity to those whose shortcomings have become all the more painfully apparent for the earlier sympathy their seven days of mourning strongly evidenced:

> Have pity upon me, have pity upon me, O ye my friends;
> For the hand of God hath touched me. (19.21)

Alone must he rise from the nadir of his solitude. Realizing this encourages him, and he expresses almost at once his strongest hope so far, impelling himself to the other extreme of the spiritual range:

> For I know *that* my Redeemer liveth,
> And *that* he shall stand at the latter *day* upon the earth: (19.25)

"Why do ye persecute me as God?" (19.22a)—this has given rise dynamically to a demand for justification, begun in a dramatic sign, "Oh that my words were now written!" (19.23), ("would that," *mi yiten,* strengthened by an asseverative, *'epho,* "indeed"). In the dynamism of his momentarily sustained confidence, Job invites the friends to identify with him:

> But ye should say, Why persecute we him,
> Seeing the root of the matter [thing] is found in me? (19.28)

And Zophar responds:

> Therefore do my thoughts cause me to answer, (20.2)

following Job's lead of beginning with himself, "I have heard the check of my reproach" (20.3). Though his approach is different, it comes to the same argument; Zophar admits the whole of Job's argument and sets the discussion to a further pitch by proceeding once more to press images on Job. These, more terrible than Bildad's, depict what happens to the "wicked man" and the "hypocrite," whom he brings back into a discussion unaffected by the force of Job's own retorts (17.5-8).

Resigning himself to the little offered by Zophar, Job declares that the friends can comfort him somewhat by simply listening to him, "Hear diligently my speech,/And let this be your consolation" (21.2). He then contents himself with directly contraverting Zophar's main burden ". . . the triumphing of the wicked *is* short,/And the joy of the hyprocite *but* for a moment" (20.5). Rather, "the wicked live,/Become old, yea, are mighty in power" (21.7). Job does not merely say this to Zophar; he confronts him with the fact as a rhetorical question. But the strain of staying on one topic, as the friends in their security too easily manage to do, taxes Job beyond his powers, and he does range back into the general vision of a mortality coming upon the good and the evil alike. Even if the evil man dies, that cannot be thought a particular punishment, since all men die; and his death may be under satisfying circumstances:

> The clods of the valley shall be sweet unto him,
> And every man shall draw after him,
> As *there are* innumerable before him. (21.33)

Job finishes this speech to the friends with a blunt question to them:

> How then comfort ye me in vain,
> Seeing in your answers there remaineth falsehood? (21.34)

Eliphaz begins the third round of speeches by taking Job's strictures as implying a release from the duty of consoling him. To shock him into the contrition that can alone put the friends at their own ease, Eliphaz embarks on a series of direct accusations, carrying the shock-tactics of Zophar even further, contradicting (22.5-7) what he had said at the very beginning (4.4-5) about Job's humane treatment of the oppressed. At this point, in discussing the evil man, he has to be echoing Bildad and Zophar, as well as Job himself. He borrows Bildad's figure (18.8-10) of the traps, and his invocation to terror (22.10); and he surprisingly abandons his elderly restraint to mimic Job's very words about God (22.17-18 repeats phrases in 21.14-16). Again he tries for balance, holding against the extravagance of Job's "iniquities infinite" (22.5) the "delight" (22.26) that shall be Job's if he "return to the Almighty" (22.23). As the repetitions of the drama are bogging the responses down, Job comes back with an expected access of bitterness (23.2) and self-defense (23.3-17). Job now abandons his appeal to the friends and centers on an effort to compose himself by surveying the dimensions of his plight. He draws the line firmly between himself and the evil man whose calamities he vies with the friends in detailing (24.1-25).

To this Bildad can reply only by assuming Job's tone of impersonal generality for himself, and by borrowing his assertions about the terror and majesty of God (25).

This frees Job for the longest of his speeches (26-31), which recapitulates by stretching still further the spiritual range of utterance. Looking backward, this long speech leaves the friends completely behind; so much so that Zophar makes no third speech at all. Looking ahead, its visionary fullness anticipates what it evokes, the comparably expanded speeches first of Elihu, then of God. In the text this self-subsistent series of utterances is called a "parable" (*mashal*, 27.1, 29.1). At its heart stands the paean to wisdom (28), a complaint insofar as it echoes Job's perplexity up to then by asserting that wisdom is nowhere it be found. The note of complaint, however, is drowned out in the note of praise, and in the certainty of the last formulation: "Behold, the fear of the Lord, that is wisdom;/And to depart from evil *is* understanding." (28.28)—a statement which abandons the attempt at definition in favor of the deliberate exercise of virtue (this in itself, though, is a definition.)

Again, everything that has been said gets not only included, but altered by the mere fact that it is repeated, the more powerfully by its presence in a broader and more interconnected stream of utterance. Job's capacity takes in a more complete destitution (30), a more awed conception of earthly riches (28) and of their uselessness to a mere possessor (27), of God's encompassing power (26), of the blessings and virtue of his past (29), of his sufferings (30), and finally of his justification (31), all in long, even, emphatic passages.

At this point of the dialogue the very volume and comprehensiveness of Job's speech demonstrates that the drama stands at a stalemate, an emotional and intellectual one. Since God later vindicates Job for what he has said, and Job has virtually finished speaking, He could presumably now intervene to justify him. There remains wanting not an intellectual justification, then, but a release, a fulfillment in terms of the emotional dynamic which has governed the grieving circle by the ash heap. And it must come from a different direction, because the possibilities in the friends have been exhausted.

And so Elihu, a young man rather than an old one, from a tribe closer to Job's than the friends are, but a person less familiar to him, intervenes. He must explain his intrusion, and he does (32), in a whole chapter, both scolding and apologizing. His own sense of dissatisfaction with the course of responses has brought him into the dialogue:

> . . . *there was* none of you that convinced Job,
> *Or* that answered his words:
> Lest ye should say, We have found out wisdom:
> God thrusteth him down, not man.
> Now he hath not directed *his* words against me:
> Neither will I answer him with your speeches. (32.12-14)

What has moved him more generally is the spirit in all men, old or young ("I said, Days should speak,/And multitude of years should teach wisdom./But *there is* a spirit in man" 32.7-8a). And he soon specifies this spirit as dwelling in his vitals, an intimate and emotive reactor:

> The spirit within me constraineth me. (32.18)

Literally, it is the spirit "in my belly," (*biṭni*, "my womb"), the word Job has himself used so often. And Elihu repeats it to specify the emotional character of his reaction in his next verse:

> Behold my belly *is* as wine *which* hath no vent;
> It is ready to burst like new bottles. (32.19)

Elihu's speeches stand midway between the unacceptable utterances of the friends on the one hand—or of Job, whom he also comes to rebuke—and on the other hand the declarations of God, which cannot be other than wholly acceptable. So his speeches share in the character of both. Dramatically they serve as a transition to the objectivity of the Almighty: he is calmer than the other friends or

Job. He echoes all their stock of points, anticipates God's majestic descriptions (though more briefly than Job had, or even Bildad), but mainly transmutes what they had said into a different order, with a different effect. It is, as I have tried to show throughout, the order of points in the speeches even more than their logicality or their justness that reveals their inner disposition, as Elihu himself comes to say toward his close:

> Teach us what we shall say unto him;
> *For* we cannot order *our speech* by reason of darkness. (37.19)

His whole speech has been based squarely on Job's premise: God's inscrutability. It is to Job he has said this, and not only ironically. It comes after a last, subtly gentle injunction to Job that will prepare him spiritually for the voice out of the whirlwind:

> Hearken unto this, O Job:
> Stand still, and consider the wondrous works of God. (37.14)

Job in his own speeches had already begun to consider them. Among these "wondrous works," in fact, must be reckoned the imminent voice of God out of the whirlwind, to which Elihu had shortly made reference, as though by way of further preparation: "God thundereth marvelously with his voice;" (37.5). Elihu's final words refer to the praise of wisdom and "fear of the lord" in Job's own speech (28.28):

> Men do therefore fear him:
> He respecteth not any *that are* wise of heart. (37.24)

(The Hebrew word for "heart" always implying both thought and emotion.)

God catches them all up with the "who" and "where" of His opening words:

> Who *is* this that darkeneth counsel . . .
> . . . .
> Where wast thou . . . . (38.2-4)

The invocation of dislocation will allow Job to locate himself and order himself like a heroic man (*ghever*, "strong man"), in response to God's command:

> Gird up now thy loins like a man; (38.3)

God offers a tremendous counterbalance, the tremendous distraction of contemplating the whole imaged creation. This invocation, at the same time, centers on Job's spiritual responsiveness because it is brought back into comparison with himself. As though to induce in Job a contemplation of the continuance of joy in the world, as against his own sorrow, the verbs "sing" and "shout" are introduced (38.7), and terms for light as against darkness, strength as against Job's weakness, and so on. God offers not only a culminating counterstatement that does not answer the initial perplexity: He produces cumulatively a sustained emotional allopathy for the man who stands always at the center of the responsive discussion. In describing Leviathan, He questions Job's "covenant" with the beasts of the field (5.23), "Will he make a covenant with thee?" (41.4). But He prepares for Job's emotional mimesis of animal creation by saying that before Leviathan "sorrow is turned [literally, "runs"] into joy." (41.22)

> Hath the rain a father?
> Or who hath begotten the drops of dew?
> Out of whose womb came the ice?
> And the hoary frost of heaven, who hath gendered it?
> The waters are hid as *with* a stone,
> And the face of the deep is frozen.
> Canst thou bind the sweet influences of Pleiades,
> Or loose the bands of Orion?
> Canst thou bring forth Mazzaroth in his season?
> Or canst thou guide Arcturus with his sons?
> Knowest thou the ordinances of heaven?
> Canst thou set the dominion thereof in the earth?
> Canst thou lift up thy voice to the clouds,
> That abundance of waters may cover thee?

> Canst thou send lightnings, that they may go,
> And say unto thee, Here we *are?*
> Who hath put wisdom in the inward parts?
> Or who hath given understanding to the heart? (38.28-36)

Not only in its form of the transcendently rhetorical question, but in the act of paralleling the content of what Job has been saying all along, God is "giving understanding to the heart" of Job. He is answering his directly negative rhetorical questions in what amounts to an affirmative. The father, the womb, the waters, the sons, the celestial bodies, stones, the weather, wisdom, the inward parts—all these items here parallel items in what Job has said, catching them up under the sway of a spiritual consistency in the divine, a consistency superior to all that precedes, as Elihu's consistency has been to the friends'. In recognition thereof does Job finally come to speak of his perceptions, and of his consequent reaction to his own person:

> I have heard of thee by the hearing of the ear;
> But now mine eye seeth thee:
> Wherefore I abhor *myself*, and repent
> In dust and ashes. (42.5-6)

Job had abhorred himself before, as his vacillations and his obsessions show. Now, more crucially, the same emotional attitude has taken the different spiritual direction induced by the counter-evocations of the divine. The internal drama has readied him for restitution into increased "blessing." Only the ritual acts remain, the friends' offerings in repentance for not having "spoken of me *the thing that is* right, as my servant Job *hath*" (42.7). Job, too, has a ritual to enact, that of the prayer for the friends into which all his responses now focus: "And the Lord turned the captivity of Job, when he prayed for his friends" (42.10a). Prayer releases him from the straitness of his circumstances, by releasing him from his exhaustion with his friends. Job is now ready in his new state for a greater prosperity: "also the Lord gave Job twice as much as he had before"

(42.10b). "So the Lord blessed the latter end of Job more than his beginning" (42.12a).

Job is an exemplary man. For the time of the book he is a dimly historical person from the age of the patriarchs nearly a millennium before, and the distance in time reinforces the human centrality of the problem which he works out. The narrative of the prologue and epilogue is noncommittal, neither suppositious as a fiction nor verifiable as a history: the distance in time obviates also the question of the historical veracity, since on that side no records can be supposed to have survived, and oral tradition would preserve—exactly!—only the essentials of the story.

So The Book of Job does not ask why Job had to suffer in order to perceive; it only dramatizes his coming to perception through suffering. He rises by himself, before God speaks, to the sense that pervades the drama: the spiritual resurgences must betoken some inner redemption through the obsessive recurrence of mortal despair. He speaks of the "redeemer" just before he speaks of his own centrality "the root" of the "thing" being "found"—as it has to be found to get beyond the patness of the friends—"in me.":

> For I know *that* my Redeemer liveth,
> And *that* he shall stand at the latter *day* upon the earth:
> And *though* after my skin *worms* destroy this *body*,
> Yet in my flesh shall I see God:
> Whom I shall see for myself,
> And mine eyes shall behold, and not another;
> *Though* my reins be consumed within me.
> But ye should say, Why persecute we him,
> Seeing the root of the matter is found in me? (19.25-28)

The ambiguity of the last clause allows the friends to be included in the "me" wherein the root is found (they may be reckoned to make the statement in fact). "After my skin" could mean at the end of the disease, or after Job's death.[35]

The "redeemer," *go'el,* is a present participle, "redeeming one." The word is used of a kinsman who makes claims for a person, and so has a technical flavor—but only a flavor. In the Prophets and the Wisdom books, *go'el* comes to be applied not to a human kinsman, but to God. Job has used the word only once before, as a verb; in his very first speech after the disease, using "claim" (if the consensus of modern commentators be taken over the older "stain") in a context of despair rather than hope, speaking of the day of his birth, "Let darkness and the shadow of death claim it" (3.5). "The shadow of death" (*tsalmaveth*) is a word occurring often in the earlier chapters, but it gradually fades away from the later chapters. The shift of emphasis on senses within the one word *go'el,* from *claim* to *redeem,* participates in, and helps create, the inner dramatic evolution of the spirit as it works its way out of, but never through and beyond, an unanswerable but transcendable question.

iii SONG OF SONGS
Love is as Strong as Death

SCENE

The Song of Songs, while of course structurally much barer than the plays of a fully articulated secular theatre, has been recognized, at least since Origen so characterized it, as being dramatic in form. Because it has an imagined scene, "courtship and marriage," its statements relate problematically to an actual scene. And this scene, in the absence of mechanisms of exclusion, would have to include actual courtship and marriage.

To what other actual scenes is this imagined scene analogous, and how? Comparative anthropological research has brought fertility rituals into the picture; on the other hand, deep devotion from early rabbis and, through Origen, Gregory the Great, Saint Bernard and Saint Theresa, down to Paul Claudel, has let the imagined scene reach out to, and be dominated by, the soul's actual search for and union with God. Even if we do not arbitrarily set these two actual scenes of reference—the anthropological and the devotional—in contradiction with one another, still, adjudicating the emphases between them becomes possible only after a close prior look at the imagined scene. And that is really so simple in its statements as to

LIBRARY ST. MARY'S COLLEGE

permit a latitude of emphasis, and of possible identifications and transpositions, between the erotic senses and the devout.

To look at the imagined scene of The Song of Songs, besides actors and spectators single and in groups, and besides amorphous episodes, it presents something that fuller dramatic works do—though Job does not—a patterned if unspecific sequence of action:

(SHE) By night on my bed I sought him whom my soul loveth:
I sought him, but I found him not.
I will rise now, and go about the city 2
In the streets, and in the broad ways
I will seek him whom my soul loveth:
I sought him, but I found him not.
The watchmen that go about the city found me: 3
To whom I said, Saw ye him whom my soul loveth?
It was but a little that I passed from them, 4
But I found him whom my soul loveth:
I held him, and would not let him go,
Until I had brought him into my mother's house,
And into the chamber of her that conceived me.
I charge you, O ye daughters of Jerusalem, 5
By the roes, and by the hinds of the field,
That ye stir not up, nor awake *my* love,
Till he please.
(THEY) Who *is* this that cometh out of the wilderness like pillars
of smoke, 6
Perfumed with myrrh and frankincense,
With all powders of the merchant?
Behold his bed, which *is* Solomon's; 7
Threescore valiant men *are* about it,
Of the valiant of Israel. (3.1-7)

The declaration of verse one leads dramatically to the declaration of verse two. By the last line of that verse something has been carried out, for the cumulative disappointment conveyed through repetition ("I sought him, but I found him not," 3.1 and 3.2). At this point the Shulamite is moved to abandon a privacy she has been cherishing. She is moved enough to ask help from others, the very guardians of the city. They represent a different order, one potentially hostile—and hostility is actualized in the different aspect of a later verse ("The watchmen that went about the city found me,/ They smote me, they wounded me;" 5.7). The guardians are not invoked here as stopping long enough even to answer. But at once union takes over from separation, and a new series occurs in the sequence, one so joyous that mere union, for the moment, is enough. The beloved is instituted into the family, with no stated erotic accompaniment other than the hint of analogous fertility in the second periphrasis for mother, "her that conceived me." At first there is beckoned to this marriage a group more friendly than the guardians, the "daughters of Jerusalem." Then the bed is surrounded on the imaginary stage by a second group, "threescore valiant men," (*giborim*).

Every one of the shifts of statement here brings in its train a shift of evoked scene: the bed (*mishkav*, sleeping place), then the streets of the city both narrow and broad, then the watchmen-confrontation, then the meeting, then the institution of the beloved in the mother's chamber, then the daughters of Jerusalem, and finally the triumphant arrival of the beloved to a royal bed (*miṭṭah*, place to recline), surrounded by his three-score warriors.

RITE

Poetic attributes that resemble the Song's are found in the marriage songs of many traditions—Egyptian, Sumerian, Assyro-Babylonian, Syro-Phoenician, among the earlier strains, and several later ones as well.[36] Furthermore, later Near Eastern rituals, Arabian and Syriac, allow us to suppose a convention of dramatized wedding celebration which involved some of the features appearing in The Song: the formalized search, the masking of the couple as king and queen, and her coronation (3.11), as well as the veiling of the bride (4:1), the presence of collective maidens, "daughters of Jerusalem," and of an honor guard of young men. Those other, formalized scenes of marriage did derive from an actual scene: a marriage did take place, and they celebrated its rites.

In a Near Eastern context of expectation, then, the imagined scene of The Song of Songs must be taken as analogous to that ritual scene, because all these elements are found not just separately but in their conventional combination. Consequently, the Song refers partly to the actual scene in which marriages may take place.

And yet nothing in the language of the Song locates it firmly as an accompaniment for a specific marriage, or for marriage in general. Moreover, the rapid changes of personnel, the insistence on the individual character of bride and groom, and the penetrating aphorisms it brings to the surface (Love is as strong as death, etc.), make the Song a larger whole than a marriage ritual can be. Of the Song, the strain of marriage celebration is the dominant one, but it is orchestrated with strains that give it a larger ambience of echo than analogous Egyptian love songs on the one hand or the Sumerian Ishtar myth on the other.

A marriage ritual in itself may refer to other rituals, most notably to seasonal rituals of fertility. Again, the crops are praised repeatedly in the Song, so that the analogy between marriage and fertility must be accounted part of its imagined scene. So, too, must reminiscences of more precisely identifiable fertility rites; the search of Ishtar and of Isis for the absent, fertile lover occurs in the same context that the search does in The Song of Songs. The term the Shulamite uses most often for her lover, *dod,* is said to echo the Babylonian "Dudu," a title of Tammuz.[37] The identification of "sister" and "bride" may recall the ritual incest of the Pharaohs, though the Song just touches on that, and the echo is a faint one, serving in this case perhaps merely to emphasize the bond of individual equality that broadens the erotic delights of these exuberant lovers.

When the Shulamite says

But my own vineyard have I not kept (1.6)

she has begun to refer to the agricultural enterprises that a seasonal ritual cosmologizes, the more so that just before she has been given an agricultural assignment in a familial setting:

> My mother's children were angry with me; [literally, "sons"]
> They made me the keeper of the vineyards; (1.6)

Still, the prevailing topic of this chapter, as of all, is personal love. And so love tends to draw all other activities into its sphere as instances of itself. Moreover, in this immediate context, the change from "vineyards" to "vineyard" insists on a distinction which induces the singular usage toward metaphor, since the plural usage already put all the literal vineyards in the Shulamite's care. The special character of the singular is emphasized in the extra turn given the possessive: not just *karmi,* "my vineyard," but *karmi shelli,* "the vineyard which is my own." The verb repeated as "keep," *naṭar,* is a rare one, used elsewhere in the Bible "only in speaking of God, who 'keeps' feelings of anger" (Jer. 3.5, 12).[38] Still, the corresponding Arabic verb gives the technical sense "care for a vine harvest," and this reading would slant the whole passage toward a strongly literal sense, though the other Biblical usages would perhaps hover in the background to reinforce the metaphorical one.

"Mother's children" (sons) establishes a full set of kin relationships, matriarchally phrased to the extent of this one formulation, the more so that later the bride wishes to bring her beloved to "my mother's house" (3.4). Just from this passage we can infer mother/children, mother-sons/mother-daughters, brothers/sister, and perhaps also a parallel set of father/sons (daughter, etc.) since failure to mention the father is significant here in itself, and especially in the light of the Song's concentration mostly on the female speaker. She, at the same time, is absorbed in seeking and praising a male who in the hinted future of delights will share in those of fertility as a father.[39]

These matriarchal relations sort well with the sedentary agricultural community implied in these verses, since anthropologists have found that such social groups tend to be matriarchal, as pastoral ones tend to be patriarchal. But the beloved, by contrast, is at once spoken of as pastoral:

Tell me, O thou whom my soul loveth,
Where thou feedest, where thou makest *thy flock* to rest at noon: (1.7)

And, just before, we had possibly a third early way of life, the nomadic, mentioned in a comparison:

> I *am* black, but comely, O ye daughters of Jerusalem,
> As the tents of Kedar, (1.5)

Indeed, the nomads of Kedar in the comparison are linked still more closely with the Shulamite by the fact that *Kedar* itself means "dark," as she has called herself (the name is possibly derived from the color of the goatshair tents that happen also to be visualized in this passage), "I am black as the tents of Dark."

The Song here touches on various social groupings—aliens of Kedar/daughters of Jerusalem, nomads/sedentary, agricultural/pastoral. Mention of these groups is kept subordinate by the associative arbitrariness with which they get picked up and dropped. They are also kept figurative by the steady contingency of their linguistic status as metaphors possible or actual, explicit or implied. (I shall return at length to this point.) Here society and family, seasonal fertility and dim terrestrial ritual, shepherd and king (. . . "As the curtains of Solomon," 1.5) are brought into the expanding orbit of a love which moves too freely in its associative recurrences to hierarchize them. Instead it operates on them transumptively. Its drama absorbs their patterns till they have become patterns no more but just verbalized expansions of delight.

> As the apple tree among the trees of the wood,
> So *is* my beloved among the sons.
> I sat down under his shadow with great delight, (2.3)

No trace is to be found here of the ritual that might *connect* shepherd and king: we are given no analogy to the year-king whose death might fertilize the crops, nor any to the human sacrifice which elsewhere in actual practise is made to a god (Moloch) who bears the name "king" (*melek*). The shepherd, who is a beloved "*dodhi*" (a word first used in 1.13), tends flocks that enter fully into the natural pleasure the drama rises to praise, so much that the shepherd's association with them merges into erotic association with the beloved:

> My beloved *is* mine, and I *am* his:
> He feedeth among the lilies (2.16; repeated 6.3)

The word for "he feedeth" is a participial form, *ha ro'eh*, the feeder, the identical word which is rendered as "shepherd" in the plural of 1.8. And in the reciprocity of the first in this pair of lines, the joyous image is applied to praise of the woman as well as the man, with a strengthening this time of the participial phrase "which feed," literally "feeding" (since the ambiguity of the noun *ro'eh* is now ruled out in the otherwise repeated expression):

> Thy two breasts *are* like two young roes that are twins,
> Which feed among the lilies. (4.5)

The exuberance of the comparison closes twice (4.2, 6.6) on the extravagant inclusion of a fertility in the flocks, whose function in the statement is wholly to subserve the perceptible delight of beauty in the bride. The analogy of her own fertility is notably left out of the comparison, as it rarely if ever is in the usual primitive marriage song, or even in such derived art songs as Catullus' two marriage poems:

> Thy hair *is* as a flock of goats, that appear from mount Gilead.
> Thy teeth *are* like a flock *of sheep that are even* shorn, which
> came up from the washing;
> Whereof every one bear twins, and none *is* barren among them.
> (4.1b-2)

The couple, through all their attributions to each other, retain their primacy as lover and beloved, male and female, both as imagined actors and in the actual reference. For the man, who changes roles most freely, "king" and "shepherd" remain subordinated to "my love." These other figures from imagined scenes, royal and pastoral, lend their attributes to enhance the primary one; love embraces in its inclusive analogies both the prosperous tending of flocks and the luxury of regal accoutrements. It is when the bride enters a chamber something like a nuptial chamber that a king is first mentioned;

> The King hath brought me into his chambers (1.4)

His luxury exists to deck out love, and for love to partake of:

> King Solomon made himself a chariot
> Of the wood of Lebanon.
> He made the pillars thereof *of* silver
> The bottom thereof *of* gold,
> The covering of it *of* purple,
> The midst thereof being paved *with* love
> For the daughters of Jerusalem.
> Go forth, O ye daughters of Zion, and behold King Solomon
> With the crown wherewith his mother crowned him
> In the day of his espousals,
> And in the day of the gladness of his heart. (3.9-11)

Solomon, standing likewise under the benevolence of a mother who crowns him for marriage, exhibits only those royal attributes which can aid love. The king does not rule, though that is what the root meaning of his name asserts as his key function, and he does not dispense wisdom, Solomon's typical function. He simply provides luxury, appearing throughout as a builder of luxurious dwellings intended mainly for marital use.[40]

Hierarchy never enters the picture in these superlatives, and so the man is easily assimilated to the king, by analogy or by exemplum, as here. The woman, too, gets superlatives; hence she is equal to what the king can delight her by providing. Does she not resemble it already?

> I *am* black, . . . as the curtains of Solomon (1.5)

The king's armies and armaments enter as defenders of the lovers, or else as analogues to another dimension of the beloved,

> Thy neck *is* like the tower of David
> Builded for an armory, (4.4)
> . . . .
> Who *is* she *that* looketh forth as the morning,
> Fair as the moon, clear as the sun,
> *And* terrible as *an army* with banners? (6.10)

What the king owns, even if it be contrasted to the possessions of the beloved, is drawn into the scene of jubilation as something fertile. He owns vineyards, of which by this last chapter we have heard much. And what he derives from them is a material that elsewhere has been used again and again to adorn the beloved:

> Solomon had a vineyard at Baal-hamon;
> He let out the vineyard unto keepers;
> Every one for the fruit thereof was to bring a thousand *pieces* of silver.
> My vinyeard, which *is* mine, *is* before me;
> Thou, O Solomon, *must have* a thousand,
> And those that keep the fruit thereof two hundred.
> Thou that dwellest in the gardens,
> The companions hearken to thy voice:
> Cause me to hear *it*. (8.11-13)

His majesty serves to gladden her when she can command it away. She is unsubjected to any diminution in the perfection of an imagined vineyard more delightful than a thousand actual ones, whatever their profit.

The shepherd brings up another king, the Pharaoh, when he begins to extol the beloved, thereby compounding the two roles while subordinating them under love:

> I have compared thee, O my love,
> To a company of horses in Pharaoh's chariots. (1.9) [literally,
> "To a mare in"]

A horse in the Biblical world is an animal of luxury and of military service, two attributes of the king that are emphasized repeatedly. Here the horse suggests not only the royal uses, but the power and size and exuberant dexterity (Job 39.21 "He paweth in the valley and rejoiceth in *his* strength") that brought about those royal uses.

Mares are fertile, but the fertility of the natural world is here deployed into a larger cosmos for those whose "soul" can "love." The Song at once proclaims the superiority of the love sought, to the produce of fertility:

> Let him kiss me with the kisses of his mouth:
> For thy love *is* better than wine. (1.2)

So much so that even abstract justice easily enters the scene:

> We will remember thy love more than wine;
> The upright love thee. (1.4)

The apples so often mentioned (2.3, 2.5, 7.8, 8.5) delight love, and neither feed it nor distract it. The fruits and the flowers all but indifferently enrich the lovers by filling out their imagined scene:

> I *am* the rose of Sharon
> *And* the lily of the valleys.
> As the lily among thorns,
> So *is* my love among the daughters.
> As the apple tree among the trees of the wood,
> So *is* my beloved among the sons. (2.1-3)

In the primacy of their love they can confound the peak of either ritualized season. As Paul Claudel says, commenting on 6.11, "A while ago it was spring, now it is autumn; the season of flowers, and now it is the season of fruits."[41] The very Hebrew calendar and its ritual observances is based on an orderly succession of agricultural events, but the Song roams exuberantly back and forth through the year.

Indeed, one of the possibilities of exuberance is a free identification of love (the word "green," *ra'anan,* is almost always used of leafy plants) with the plain fertility it always surpasses. It does so by its freedom of dramatic statement, in the very identification:

> Behold, thou *art* fair, my beloved, yea pleasant:
> Also our bed *is* green. (1.16)

The word rendered "also," *'aph,* is really an emphatic, "indeed our bed is green." The lovers are empowered to say so in the free arbitrariness of transritual identification.

SCRIPTURE

Paramount in the Song are the lovers, and for them their love is paramount. Where in Near Eastern traditions, as in others, fertile people bring about fertile crops, here the fertility of seasons and generations is drawn into another order, one at once larger and simpler. "Also our bed is green"; among the occasions of hymeneal rejoicing stands the incorporation of similitude to the fertile crops.

Indeed, the Song's largeness of love admits of the powerful elaborations of sexuality into theology that are touched on in the Old Testament (Isaiah 61.10, etc.), and developed later in the New. Christ is to the Church as the bridegroom to the bride; and then, reading the equation back again to the second degree: the bridegroom is to the bride as Christ to the Church, "For the husband is the head of the wife, even as Christ is the head of the Church: and he is the savior of the body" (Ephesians 5.23). Origen's expansions about the Song into an allegory formal (the Soul and God) and historical (Christ and the Church), remain in the spirit of the Song, and St. Theresa's delicate series of homilies on it manages to avoid setting spirit against flesh by nuancing a distance from its actual words.

In the context of the Old Testament itself, without moving ahead to these developments, the sexual relation, both actually in Proverbs and metaphorically in the prophets, bears religious significances other than the automatic, magical one of inducing the order of physical nature to remain benign. And we are still learning how in a person's sex do flesh and spirit converge; how one's identity finds expression in his sexual bearing, both direct and sublimated. Virtually omnipresent in the unfolding drama of our lives, sexuality comes clear as interacting with those deepest impulses to which religion lays final claim.

The Song sets out that interaction within the sphere of praise for sexuality. To begin with, it is imagined to be spoken at the acme of erotic arousal and expectation, when all the heightened senses bring themselves into play for a fulfillment in which the personal and the typical also converge by fortifying one another into triumphant identity.

The identity is accomplished through the indirection of a language (rather than a coition) itself at once copious and veiled by indirection. Just as the divine name occurs in the Song only once, and then in the hint of an epithet ("flame" [of God], 8.7), so coition, the center of desire in the poem, is veiled by circumlocution, by metaphor, or by roundabout description of the delights of love play. While the poem is clear on its bodily preoccupation from the outset ("Let him kiss me with the kisses of his mouth," 1.2), it is not till the penultimate chapter that a term heavily weighted toward physical lovemaking occurs, in a nominalized plural:

> How fair and how pleasant art thou, O love, for delights! (7.6)

While the man has been praising the beloved, and invoking her, this vocative puts his "love" into the abstract, the act of feeling love for another person, "'*ahavah*," as she has earlier called him her '*ahavah* (2.7). That affection brings in its train *ta'anughim* ("delights"), literally "languorous and dainty pleasures," a rare noun formed from a verb meaning "be dainty," "take exquisite delight," "make merry," and cognate with an Arabic verb that carries a strong erotic tinge. For all this, the term "'*ahavah*" is itself so abstract that it has moved many commentators to the desperate strait of emendation.[42]

The Song asserts itself the more emphatically for altering so profoundly the connection between sexual action and religion expressed in the prophets, where the personal immediately amplifies itself into the public. Only in passing does Jeremiah have God make a direct reference to the sort of marriage celebration the Song dramatizes:

> Behold, I will cause to cease out of this place
> In your eyes, and in your days, the voice of mirth, and the
> voice of gladness,

> The voice of the bridegroom, and the voice of the bride.
> (Jer. 16.9)

In the course of Israel's deprivations, this particular one signalizes the country's separation from the harmony it has violated by "playing the whore" (Jer. 3.1). The conjugal metaphor that in the prophets so frequently represents the relation between God and Israel, harnesses the emotional force of marriage, and all its bodily bond in "one flesh" (Gen. 2.24) to demonstrate the enormity of a departure from God. In Jeremiah's accusation, an order of nature is violated, and the familial basis of society, and the principle of trust between the two kinds of humanity, the sexes; and the very economic support of the woman, as well as the nexus of ties which allow her to esteem herself and not have to feel "shame." Adultery, the violation of marriage, more than marriage itself, dominates this metaphor in the prophets, whose sorrowing occasions allow them to contemplate only in the distance of violation what a true marriage should be, even when a Hosea tries to enact a restoration of conjugal order in the personal sphere by marrying a prostitute. The Song touches on "jealousy" (*qin'ah*, 8.6) only to hint at a divine connection, and only to reinforce the exuberance about order. The order in the Song is so great that it can move at will among the stages of erotic involvement: it confounds first love, betrothal, marriage, and lifelong fidelity while the prophets, as Neher[43] points out, keep the stages distinct, adding to them the series of separation: seduction, adultery, repudiation, prostitution, divorce, death of children, widowhood. For these last in the Song there is no room.

Israel does enter the incantation of the Song, through redolent place names: Jerusalem, Sharon, En-Gedi, Hermon. Yet the names are either so apparent in their signification or so purely geographical in their association that it would take considerable ingenuity to follow the Targum, as commentators from Origen to Robert have done, and read the Song as the sort of public, historical assertion that is so clear in the prophets:

> How is the faithful city
> Become a harlot!

It was full of judgment;
Righteousness lodged in it;
But now murderers. (Isaiah 1.21)

Isaiah makes the very terms of the Song into a public parable by coupling vineyard and "my beloved" (*dodhi*, occurring in this form twenty-six times in the Song but only three other times throughout the Bible; in other forms, more often in the Song, still, than in all uses elsewhere in scripture):

Now will I sing to my well-beloved
A song of my beloved touching his vineyard.
My well-beloved hath a vineyard
In a very fruitful hill: . . .
And now, O inhabitants of Jerusalem, and men of Judah,
Judge, I pray you, betwixt me and my vineyard . . .
For the vineyard of the Lord of hosts *is* the house of Israel,
And the men of Judah his pleasant plant: (Isaiah, 5.1-7)

The Song, in its statements at least, offers us no such equations as the last ones here. Remarkably in the Bible, it refers its transformations of scenic confrontation and assertion back again to itself; the world of nature is funded into love, and so is the world of men, not the other way around. If love is so ineffable as to include the divine name (this must be so for the Song to be canonical), in that ineffability it does not emerge into those namings of "Lord" and "God" with which all the other books of the Bible abound. Instead, and again remarkably, it is of the beloved's name that the Song speaks, "Thy name *is as* ointment poured forth" (1.3).

The place-names of geography do not expand into historical and public association, as they do elsewhere in the canon. Lebanon and Damascus, like Carmel, Heshbon, and Bath-rabbim, serve mainly to exalt the Shulamite:

Thine eyes *like* the fishpools in Heshbon, by the gate of Bath-rabbim:
Thy nose *is* as the tower of Lebanon which looketh toward Damascus.
Thine head upon thee *is* like Carmel (7.4-5).

Even the familial, in this celebration of instituting a family, does not come into a primary place of reference. The actual marriages in the Old Testament narratives quickly find their erotic appeal dissolved into the tribal functions: Rachel and Bathsheba both become matrons, anxious about the welfare of their children. Dwelling on sexuality as the Song does, is spoken of elsewhere in its negative character, as tempting to idolatry, the worship of Ammon; or else, if it persists, it insinuates itself into the self-destructions of adultery, as Proverbs continually warns:

> So she caught him and kissed him,
> *And* with an impudent face said unto him,
> *I have* peace offerings with me;
> This day have I paid my vows.
> Therefore came I forth to meet thee,
> Diligently to seek thy face, and I have found thee.
> I have decked my bed with coverings of tapestry,
> With carved *works*, with fine linen of Egypt.
> I have perfumed my bed
> With myrrh, aloes, and cinnamon.
> Come, let us take our fill of love until the morning:
> Let us solace ourselves with loves.
> For the goodman *is* not at home,
> He is gone a long journey. . . .
> He goeth after her straightway
> As an ox goeth to the slaughter, . . .
> Her house *is* the way to hell,
> Going down to the chambers of death. (Prov. 7.13-27)

Here many of the erotic inducements of the Song are produced by "a woman/*With* the attire of a harlot, and subtile of heart" (Prov. 7.10), and the delight lures to self-destruction.

Moreover, Proverbs reads the personal marital relation into a context of good management and prudence:

> Who can find a virtuous woman?
> For her price *is* far above rubies.
> The heart of her husband doth safely trust in her,
> So that he shall have no need of spoil.

"ravish the heart" (*libavtini*), a verb repeated at once for further intensification:

> Thou-hast-ravished-my-heart, my sister, *my* spouse;
> Thou-hast-ravished-my-heart with one of thine eyes,
> With one chain of thy neck. (4.9) [I have hyphenated all the words used to render the one verb *libavtini*.]

The dimness of the speakers, whose voices alone bring them into the imagined scene, throws what they utter into relief. All the single persons named as present, king or Solomon or shepherd, queen or Shulamite, sister or bride or beloved, come to unity as primarily male or female, primarily lover or beloved. The freedom of their roles testifies to the exuberance of their love.

Otherwise, the only dramatic movement presented in the Song is that from isolation to union, or the other way around.

The other groups present—the daughters of Jerusalem, the warriors, the queens and concubines (8.6), the guards, the "shepherds" (1.8), the "friends" (5.1)—all act exclusively to help or hinder the lovers' union. Other, allegorized motives can be attributed to the speakers, single or choral, as the force of the love reaches out inclusively, but the central energy is an erotic one. It gets the first speaker, the Shulamite (presumably), quickly from the third person to the more intimate second.

> The Song of songs, which *is* Solomon's.
> Let him kiss me with the kisses of his mouth: 2
> For thy love *is* better than wine.
> Because of the savor of thy good ointments 3
> Thy name *is as* ointment poured forth,
> Therefore do the virgins love thee.
> Draw me, we will run after thee: 4
> The King hath brought me into his chambers:
> We will be glad and rejoice in thee,
> We will remember thy love more than wine:
> The upright love thee.
> I *am* black, but comely, O ye daughters of Jerusalem. . . . 5
> Tell me, O thou whom my soul loveth, 7

Where thou feedest, where thou makest *thy flock* to rest at noon:
For why should I be as one that turneth aside
By the flocks of thy companions?
If thou know not, O thou fairest among women 8
Go thy way forth by the footsteps of the flock.

The designation of the man's identity, the very name that never emerges from him in the course of so many evocations, acts like perfume on her—and also, she asserts, on the other young women. "Thy name is as ointment poured forth." She, too, is never given a name other than (probably) her place of origin when he is trying to place her, "Return, return, O Shulamite" (6.13). When she speaks triumphantly of her own identity, it is in a metaphor that merges her with love, as something fertile, beautiful, fragrant, and delicate with color, amid something that is none of these: she is a flower in the desert (the "I" being emphatic): I *am* the rose of Sharon (2.1).

At the beginning the persons change freely, as throughout, but their concern does not: in 1.4 above, the Shulamite cannot be detached from the "we" who speak; nor is she lost in this band of daughters of Jerusalem (it might be), who might in turn be the same as the "virgins" of 1.3. Her lover, at first distanced in the language ("let him kiss me") (1.2) if not absent, enters the imagined scene to be asked a question by 1.7. He speaks by 1.8, to answer both halves of her question, referring her back to herself and praising her at the same stroke "If thou know not, O thou fairest among women,/Go thy way" (1.8). His gentle command, followed as it is by more extravagant praise, has the dramatic effect of banter: she must be presumed to know, even if his presence alone now provides her with the knowledge.

In his statement, as the King James Version does not render it, a stronger reference to her person is made, "If thou know not *for thyself* (*lak*)." This reference is still stronger in the Septuagint, which gives it as "know thyself," (*gnos seauten*), so that Origen takes the expression in the Socratic sense,[45] as does Paul Claudel,

" 'If you do not know thyself,' and you would not know it if I did not tell it to you, if I did not confront you with your first principle (*cause*)."[46] Even if later commentators are right in revising the Septuagint-Vulgate reading of *lak*, the forcefulness of the expression which induced a possible overtranslation shades the lover's words into the Socratic command. The beloved comes to self-realization only through this other. Later, when he "whom my soul loveth" (1.7), has withdrawn, her soul is gone out:

> My soul went out [*naphshi yats'ah*] when he withdrew (5.6)[47]

The person of the lover comes to fullness in the presence of the other fulfilled person, and comes to the identity of joy only in the joy of bodily identity. In his eyes she can praise herself as well as himself, but only he can call her "perfect" (*thammathi*, 5.2, 6.9, "my undefiled"). The roles of indirect heightening may even reach out to domesticate exoticism, if the black Shulamite has a strange look. And only in the Song, of all Scripture, is a royal term ("prince's daughter, 7.1) applied to any woman who is not explicitly Oriental.

Marriage, lifelong marriage, is what the lovers are approaching in their transports:

> Set me as a seal upon thine heart,
> As a seal upon thine arm:
> For love *is* strong as death . . .
> Many waters cannot quench love,
> Neither can the floods drown it: (8.6-7)

At the same time, the speeches treat the formal context of marriage freely enough to permit that central union only the emphasis of a ground for realizing its pleasure. The "bride" (KJ "spouse") is named, in the lover's transports of delight, as one among the many roles the Shulamite can play, though this chief one gets named again and again once it occurs:

> Come with me from Lebanon, *my* spouse, . . .
> Thou hast ravished my heart, my sister, *my* spouse . . .
> How fair is thy love, my sister, *my* spouse! . . .

> Thy lips, O *my* spouse, drop *as* the honeycomb: . . .
> A garden inclosed *is* my sister, *my* spouse; . . . (4.9-12)
> I am come into my garden, my sister, *my* spouse (5.1)

Still, once the lover has reached this extreme of naming, he goes back to it no more. His transport shows here in another extreme, that of repeatedly coupling "bride" with an intimate familial role, "sister." The coupling of these names overthrows the incest taboo, as well as perhaps suggesting the royal exoticism of an Egyptian dynastic custom. The Shulamite had earlier (3.4) spoken of bringing the beloved into her mother's house, so feminizing her perceptions as she fulfills her feminine identity that she dreamily declares the patriarchal society of Israel into its tribal opposite. In the freedom of their interactive praise patriarchy can be confounded into matriarchy, and endogamy heightened past taboo into (imagined) incest. All intimacies, even forbidden ones, and all familial arrangements, even impossible ones, shower their attributes on the pair whom erotic joy expands into the multiple possibilities and heightened identities of union.

SONG

The song superlative among songs, "The Song of Songs", vests its incantatory utterances of dramatic posture wholly in its language: there are no stage directions, no narrative tags or frames of contrasted prose as in Job, and no names for the speakers other than those they utter of one another or themselves. In their imagined scene they speak, purely and simply, in words whose richness of association comes back round to their central delight. If Isaiah speaks of a vineyard, as in the passage quoted above, it gets located immediately in the dynamic structure of the relations among Israel and God, Israel and prophet, past, present, and future. The eschatological "burden" of the prophet makes the vineyard a typological one, whose fertility or lack of it connects intimately with the life of a literal farmer, with Israel's rightness before God, with God's pleasure. In the dim reaches of the prophet's temporal perspectives, all other vineyards from Naboth's to St. Luke's (20.9-16), all other vines from the tree of Jesse to the person of Christ ("I am the true vine," John 15.1), may be brought into the reference. In its uncertain distance from other parts of the canon, and in its self-referential dramatic structure, the Song does not indicate a typological reading (though neither does it discourage one; and its presence in the canon as well as its associative metaphorical strain may be taken indirectly to invite typological association).

Whether the vineyard that the Shulamite tends (1.6) is real or metaphorical, it belongs fully to the scene of her love, and our uncertainty rests only with placing the particular scene at this point in her body or in the fields of her home. Our uncertainty about "the little foxes, that spoil the vines," meets the same limits, and those limits allow delectation within them: "For our vines *have* tender grapes (2.15). / My beloved *is* mine, and I am his (2.16." The significance is the same when the vine is clearly metaphorical, as in the first of these verses, or even when it is clearly literal, as in the last:

> Now also thy breasts shall be as clusters of the vine,
> And the smell of thy nose like apples; . . .
> Come, my beloved, let us go forth into the field;
> Let us lodge in the villages.
> Let us get up early to the vineyards;
> Let us see if the vine flourish, *whether* the tender grape appear.
> (7.8-12)

The words are so rich with association that each of them rises into the splendid euphoria of the spoken enactment, the more so that the richness comes back round to the love. The "garden" is the beloved herself, and no distant reference to Eden enters necessarily. Indeed, even if Eden is construed to enter, that reference would scarcely add more than a faint cosmic assertion to the condition of realized delight. The Song has already (imaginatively) achieved the condition of Eden without giving that condition a location in space or time. Eden is everywhere, because the lovers are everywhere to each other; from this garden they are not yet to be imagined as excluded, though in the preliminary separation the beloved is a "garden inclosed" (4.12). They are mortal, but in the preoccupation of the poem they resemble Adam and Eve in not turning their thoughts toward the death that banishment brought; "Love *is* strong as death" (8.6).

Strongly recurrent in this rich verse are the words of wide connotation—"vine," "garden," "rose," "horse," "sheep," "chariot," "shepherd," "king," "valley," "river," "flock," "house," "tower," "banner," "fruit." Words of narrower lexical connotation carry enriched associations of luxury and fertility: "nard," "pomegranate," "roe," "myrrh," "frankincense," "gold," "silver," "dew," "beryl," "spices," "raven." The speeches move from rich word to rich word in a heady atmosphere of richness. The very place-names have enriched physical connotations for having, on the whole, dim historical ones; not ever directly mentioned is any place more distant from Israel than Damascus. Often, as in Sharon (plain), Kedar (black), and En-Gedi (spring of the kid), the place name turns out to be just another loaded word in disguise; a richness always the same is displaced onto geography and returns in a space everywhere eroticized into an utterance always joyous. The exuberance spills over into the doublings of synonymity—there are many words for "beloved" in the song, metaphoric and literal; and even many words for "bed." A word's relevant associations pile up (without referring to a usual biblical structure of figuration) the moment we dwell on them, as Paul Claudel[48] piles up associations on hyacinth,[49] "a stone whose characteristic is to present the mixture of a double coloration, say blue and red;" and on "ivory," "which resumes the ideas of inalterable purity, unshakeable solidity, total homogeneity, and at the same time of something elaborated by life itself. Such does it stand, without wrinkle and

LIBRARY ST. MARY'S COLLEGE

perfectly smooth, the tower of ivory.[50] The tower of ivory is the neck of the beloved (7.4). But everything is hers, one way or another, literally or metaphorically.

The delight the lovers take in eulogizing each other emerges in the eloquence of their enriched articulations. A speaker amplifies these in rapid succession, demonstrating the emotion behind each word through the intensity of associativeness in the word chosen, in the closeness of one rich word to another. Even the far-fetchedness of many metaphors testifies to the speaker's leap into an expression as extravagant as the transport of which the words alone tell us. Sometimes the excitement will bring the metaphor trailing along behind in a breathless confusion:

> The voice of my beloved! behold, he cometh
> Leaping upon the mountains, skipping upon the hills.
> My beloved is like a roe or a young hart. (2.8-9)

If he skips on hills and mountains then he must be (the parallelism provides the framework for correspondences in continuation) a roe or a young hart, animals whose other rich metaphoric associations (smoothness, youth, free impulsiveness, etc.) all add up to the one entrancing and all-embracing quality: he is good for love. In a while she enjoins him tenderly to be what he already has been said to be.

> Turn, my beloved,
> And be thou like a roe or a young hart
> Upon the mountains of Bether. (2.17)

She, too, in the convergences of mutual praise, is given a more far-fetched attribution. She resembles a roe at rest:

> Thy two breasts *are* like two young roes that are twins,
> Which feed among the lilies. (4.5)

Love takes by giving and gives by taking; giving increases, and does not diminish. So the breasts, which feed offspring and please the lover, are said to feed themselves, to feed themselves in the midst of flowers which may image the body whence they spring as instances of fertility (twins are associated with fertility: 4.2 and 6.6) as well as of beauty, the beauty of the very flower she named when extolling her own beauty: "I *am* the rose of Sharon, / *And* the lily of the valleys." (2.1). At that point he responds at once by repeating her image less extravagantly: "As the lily among thorns, / So *is* my love among the daughters" (2.2). This response is still a full one, since in repeating her second flower, the "lily," he reproduces the antithetic parallelism of her first: a rose in the desert of Sharon stands out by delightful contrast, just as a lily does among thorns.

At the very end, in the fullness of anticipation, he heightens the richness of the animal image and the mountain image by adding a third image, that of the spices abundantly named throughout, spices storing up the scent to be found naturally in roses or lilies:

> Make haste, my beloved,
> And be thou like to a roe or to a young hart
> Upon the mountains of spices. (8.14)

Here are given not only a metaphor for the beloved, but, as often in the delicate indirection of erotic language, a *double-entendre* for erotic play. Usually the *double-entendre* is so delicate as to leave some doubt about its presence at a specific point. But more generally, erotic play is always somehow in question, because the conative direction of all the speeches moves dramatically as an approach toward it. More particularly, the *double-entendre* is always a possibility, because at some times the erotic strain is unambiguously clearer than at others:

> I sleep, but my heart waketh:
> *It is* the voice of my beloved that knocketh, *saying,*
> Open to me, my sister, my love, my dove, my undefiled:
> For my head is filled with dew,
> *And* my locks with the drops of the night.
> I have put off my coat; how shall I put it on?
> I have washed my feet; how shall I defile them?
> My beloved put in his hand by the hole *of the door,*
> And my bowels were moved for him.

> I rose up to open to my beloved;
> And my hands dropped *with* myrrh
> And my fingers *with* sweet smelling myrrh,
> Upon the handles of the lock. (5.2-5)

Is a rise of tender anticipation dallying with erotic reference in "head filled with dew"? If this is not clear, if there is some doubt about "hole of the door," there is none about "my bowels," or about the far-fetched metaphor that has the sweetness of anticipated caresses distilled into palpable fragrance, "my hands dropped with myrrh." The story underlying these dramatic speeches clearly has the lovers move toward coition. Hence the invocation preceding the above speech must be taken for a heady *double-entendre*:

> Let my beloved come into his garden,
> And eat his pleasant fruits.
> I am come into my garden, my sister, *my* spouse:
> I have gathered my myrrh with my spice;
> I have eaten my honeycomb with my honey;
> I have drunk my wine with my milk: (4 16-5.1)

Satisfaction here spills over into amplified utterance, one enriched by *double-entendres* whose refere.ıce to fertility magic is distant—and is therefore itself, in still another dimension, metaphorical.

In the general pattern of search and finding that the Song presents, the very arbitrariness of what the moment may bring increases delight; unexpectedness creates added pleasure. *Double-entendre* expresses, suddenly, in its fluent delicacy of tone, the access of delight. In those moments of separation, when the Shulamite's words dramatize her as wholly preoccupied with absence, when she cannot even conjure up the beloved in her momentary imagination, then is her speech the most earnest—in this poetry, most un-nuanced and unmetaphorical:

> I charge you, O ye daughters of Jerusalem,
> By the roes, and by the hinds of the field,
> That ye stir not up, nor awake *my* love
> Till he please. (2.7, 3.5)

Here no erotic possibility is in view, though the lover himself is presumably present. And the language is correspondingly both explicit and subdued. But usually the dramatic statement moves into erotic possibility, and the dynamism of this approach opens the language into metaphor and *double-entendre*.

The Song runs in its general fluidity along a scale from literalness to "absolute" metaphor. For the last, in a metaphor like:

> His head *is as* the most fine gold; (5.11)

there are no specific correspondences, however far-fetched, between vehicle ("fine gold") and tenor ("head"). If the beloved is precious, his whole self is precious; and synedoche is ruled out by the context, which gives a rapid series of "head," "locks," "eyes," "cheeks," "lips," "hands," "belly," "legs," "countenance," and "mouth." And if he is beautiful in some general sense as gold is, many of the other metaphors at this point are visually specific. This particular metaphor sets out not so much itemizable correspondences between the head and gold as a heightened world in which all the members are superlatives,[51] resembling one another most essentially by their membership in that world. Since this world tends to draw its items from the luxury of the king's existence, "Solomon" in the poem may be taken not only dramatically for a role which the lover is declared to assume, but thereby metaphorically as a kind of absolute and doubled superlative: a superlative man (the beloved) is a king, a superlative king is Solomon.[52] With a possible *double-entendre*, Solomon is a king given to eroticizing beauty; but, again, we may possibly rule him out by taking the lovers as greater than this specially sympathetic double superlative, through their fidelity to one another:

> As a piece of a pomegranate *are* thy temples within thy locks.
> There are threescore queens, and fourscore concubines,
> And virgins without number.

My dove, my undefiled is *but* one;
She *is* the *only* one of her mother,
She *is* the choice *one* of her that bare her.
The daughters saw her, and blessed her;
Yea, the queens and the concubines, and they praised her.
(6.7-9)

This passage is, consistently, so unqualified in its praise of the beloved, that we cannot take the lover's statement about queens and concubines, with some commentators, as in any sense concessive, "They may be numerous, but this isolated commoner is at least mine." While the King James translators edit concessiveness in by adding, "but," to the Hebrew, "My dove, my undefiled is (*but*) one," they do always give us the cue by italicizing their additions. Here in their conjecture they err with many. In this very line, "undefiled," as above, means also "perfect," and "without blemish" (*thammathi*). The queens and concubines and virgins are given in round numbers, and set off against the "choice" one whom here they end by praising. Again, she is immediately said to have attributes still greater than the royal ones, embracing cosmically the beauty of one heavenly body and the clarity of another, along with the awareness of the early day. In her range of emotional evocation she also possesses a terror akin to that of the king's armies:

Who *is* she *that* looketh forth as the morning,
Fair as the moon, clear as the sun,
And terrible as *an army* with banners? (6.10)

In the flourish of their dramatized "inventiveness," the speeches tend toward the metaphorical end of a scale running from literal to absolute metaphor. They gain delight, and embody delight, by rising so often into whole flights of similar metaphor. One metaphor ("emblematic parallelism") leads to another, and to still others ("staircase parallelism").

At times the associative freedom tends to dwell on a delight of expression, once a delight has been found. Or the freedom enjoys its utterance by running up and down the scale, from literal to metaphorical and back again:

> As the apple tree among the trees of the wood,
> So *is* my beloved among the sons.
> I sat down under his shadow with great delight
> And his fruit *was* sweet to my taste. (2.3)

The "apple" (tree), "*thapuaḥ*" runs quickly from the singular and clearly metaphorical to this plural which, on the designative surface at least, is clearly literal:

> Stay me with flagons, comfort me with apples [*tapuḥim*]. (2.5)

In this movement, the same word *thapuaḥ* now designates the fruit and not the tree, and it offers other delights than those of a metaphorical "shadow."

The next shadows to be mentioned are explicitly literal:

> Until the day break, and the shadows flee away,
> Turn, my beloved,
> And be thou like a roe or a young hart
> Upon the mountains of Bether. (2.17)

These literal shadows are also mobile, whereas that of the apple tree moves so slowly as to provide its "great delight" by seeming stationary. But in whatever aspect they appear, whether one shadow or many, literal or metaphorical, all the aspects that may be uttered or seen have the single, unavoidable function of being benign. They point always one way, toward love, as the many geographical metaphors (Kedar, Heshbon, Tirzah, En-gedi, etc.), by their repetition, persistently suggest identifying the contour of the country with the body of the beloved, at least to the extent that they possess common attributes. But the associativeness of the statements does not encourage our reading the metaphor the other way, from the body of the beloved to Israel. Love, in this respect too, fills out the whole imagined scene. When the language runs through the literal-metaphorical scale, in large compass or in small, it comes back round to the dominance of Love:

> King Solomon made himself a chariot
> Of the wood of Lebanon.
> He made the pillars thereof *of* silver
> The bottom thereof *of* gold,
> The covering of it *of* purple,
> The midst thereof being paved *with* love,
> For the daughters of Jerusalem.
> Go forth, O ye daughters of Zion, and behold King Solomon
> With the crown wherewith his mother crowned him
> In the day of his espousals,
> And in the day of the gladness of his heart. (3.9-11)

We have other metaphorical chariots (1.9, 6.12). Only if this one has some metaphorical force, can the "love" with which it is "paved" be the literal love[53] of the couple. Or if the chariot is literal, then the love would be some metaphoric extension. But in any case, and through the circle of possibilities that do not so much cancel each other out as amplify each other, we are brought round again to the crowned bridegroom and the gladness of his heart—whose identification with Solomon can, in turn, be run through the same literal-metaphoric cycle.

Parallelism, the form of the verse, provides a structure of expectation into which these identifications can be built. When the speaker dwells on them, he merely prolongs the parallelism into a near-strophic run. The parallelism tends toward emblem: the metaphor has a syntactic (paralleled) function of identification as well as an imaging and connotation-broadening one:

a (1)	b (2)	c (3)
A bundle of myrrh	*is* my well-beloved	unto me;

d (2) e (4) f (5) g (6)
He shall lie all night betwixt my breasts.

h (2) i (3) j (1)
My beloved *is* unto me *as* a cluster of camphire

k (7) l (7?)
In the vineyards of En-gedi.
m (8; 1?) n (2) o (8; 1?)
Behold, thou *art* fair, my love; behold, thou *art* fair;

p (9) q (10)
Thou *hast* doves' eyes.
r (8; 1) s (2) t (2)
Behold, thou *art* fair, my beloved, yea, pleasant;
u (11) v (12)
Also our bed *is* green (1.13-16)

Instead of using the more common system, I have lettered every element sequentially, and numbered the repetitions. There is some doubt about these, though. More of them could be classified together. In fact, all of them could be placed under three headings, "my love," "desirable," and "something desirable," the three themselves classifiable into one as equivalents for one another. More specifically, however, En-gedi is both in antithesis to "vineyard," since the place named is a desert; and in synonymy with it, since the name of the place means "spring of the kid," a fertile place. This association of garden and fountain, each a kind of fertility, runs as a motif through the Song, converging at 4.15 in a paralleled synonymy:

> A fountain of gardens, a well of living waters,
> And streams from Lebanon.

Thus do the richnesses enrich each other. The enrichment intensifies so fully that the parallelism rises to identity toward the end here: "behold thou art fair," gets a threefold repetition. But it also intensifies freely, and the final member is not parallel at all, except in the most general way, to the verse paired with it, though "bed" names what is implied throughout, and "green" may be taken (I have not so numbered it, however) as parallel to "vineyards." The verse runs the gamut from the maximum of parallelism, identity, to the minimal correspondence between the halves of the last pair.

Now the normal case of parallelism is a symmetrical correspondence between two or three members of one verse and an equal number of the next. (I now employ a more usual notation):

A B
He looketh forth at the windows,
a b
Showing himself through the lattice (2.9)

Under these normal circumstances, each line of a pair divides into halves, and the halves roughly correspond, to repeat one another: "looketh forth" roughly matches "Showing himself," as "at the windows" does "through the lattice."

But generally such normal correspondences are far enough apart in the Song that the verse creates no such usual expectation. Nor are the departures complicated or compounded the way they are in Job and the prophets. Characteristically the parallelism "simplifies" by identifying within one line the first half in some way very fully with the second, as in the frequent "emblematic" parallelism, when often the emblem is not put in the second line of a pair, but, rather, is stated at once in the second half of the given line. The movement is toward not symmetry but identity. So, in the lines quoted above (1.13-16), we have only about half as many numbered items (1-12) as we have lettered phrases (a-v), and all the numbered items can be reclassified into three, or again simply into one.

This identity reinforces itself, in the quoted series as often throughout the Song, by the absence of a more usual symmetry: no first line in a pair neatly matches a second line, unless an emblem be taken for a match. But there are only two possible cases of such an emblem in the second line of a pair: *p-q*, and *u-v;* and the other two cases of emblem, *a* and *j-k-l,* occur syntactically (though the second does run over) within one line. We have to skip a line to get symmetry: *a-b-c-* corresponds to *h-i-j,* invertedly (1-2-3 against 2-3-1). And here, once we are given symmetry, we at once get identity as well: the Hebrew terms are identically *dodhi,* "my beloved" and *li* "to me" in both cases. In the other case of symmetry gained by skipping a line, *m-n-o* with *r-s-t* (giving 8-2-8 and 8-2-2), we get the identity between *m* and *r* tripled by the identity with *o*, this tripling in the identical parallelism gained by repeating at once within one line (*m-o*) what is to be repeated formally between a pair (*m-r*). As though to insist on the form from which this is a departure, the elements coupled with them modify the assertion of identity into a more usual symmetry, "my love" (*ra'yathi*) with the word already twice given here (*b, h*), "my beloved" (*dodhi*), and "fair" with "pleasant," though again "fair" is given three times, each time in the strophic commencement of a phrase, "*hinneka yapheh*," "behold thou *art* fair."

All the identities return to the lovers, to the love that they embody for one another. In the fluency with which love has endowed them, in the outspokenness to which their urgency for one another is dramatized as having led them, the form of their utterance holds them always to the same declaration. So it frees them for a banter which will turn serious, or for a near-lament (the *qinah*[54] or lamentation-verse comes up now and then) which will turn to joy. All finally merge in the spoken praise that accompanies an ultimate and silent union.

SEEKING AND FINDING

The degree of individual metaphor in any one verse of the Song, the presence and modality of general metaphor or allegory in the whole, and the indeterminate distance of the Song's assertion from the rest of the canon to which it has belonged for millenia, are all related problems.

But, however, the Song is finally taken, we must attend to the sequence in it because of the dramatic form implied.[55] in its assignment of verses to more than a single voice. For, however much we reduce it, with Herder and his successors, to the marriage songs whose forms it adopts, it cannot be broken up into separate units like Psalms or Proverbs, nor is there much ground for assigning portions of it to different writers, as with Isaiah. Leaving aside its clear thematic departures from all other similar songs in the Near East and elsewhere, its recurrences link it into an order. Nor do its breaks fragment it, since every break can be assigned to the clear changes of voice from the fourth verse on.

Still there is no necessity to confect for the action some plot more specific than in fact it offers us. The scholars who have done this, Renan and others, act much like a psychological subject in a thematic apperception test who will produce a whole family history when shown, say, the picture of a young boy sitting with a woman in a room that a man is entering. Given "king," "Solomon," and "daughters of Jerusalem," "shepherd," "warriors," "mother's children," "guard," "queens," "beloved," and "Shulamite," they then arrange a plot according to their fancy, often rearranging the order or the very letters of the text when it resists.

But, however we dispose of its ultimate assertions, the immediate emphasis of the Song is clearly on love, on love as invested in the body, heightened because of an approach to (something like a) marriage. The Song is articulated through a form that allows such speech only under special conditions, and yet at the same time it is often given the indirection of metaphor for a similar reason.

In its sequence, the tonic note is given at once, more literally than in any of the elaborations to follow: "Let him kiss me with the kisses of his mouth" (1.2). And it stays with remarkable evenness in the range of this tone.

In Psalms, the prophets, Job, the verse enlivens its sequence into a range of moods, moving quickly and profoundly from hope to despair, from sorrow to joy, from self-deprecation to self-exaltation, and back again. In the sequence of The Song of Songs, so strongly does its leading impulse dominate the verse that this diversity is absorbed into one all-embracing mood. What sounds somewhat like despair rises instantly to hope, incipient sorrow blossoms as joy. The joy of love never leaves the bride, when she is so absorbed in seeking love, and when finding love is so close at hand. The paralleling repetitions saturate the Song emotionally in the mood of a vivacious affirmation, a mood sustained through all its unusual variety of metres and abrupt shifts of person.

From beginning to end the lovers go from seeking each other to finding each other. But this action does not move in a straight line from separation to union: it leaps, in impulsions of voiced desire, from anticipated joy to actualized joy, and back again. Any speech may discover itself anywhere on the circle of seeking and finding. The very first one, which speaks of seeking, also enters imaginatively into finding: "Let him kiss me with the kisses of his mouth" (1.2). And the Shulamite already knows so well why she utters her injunction that her rapture at the outset transcends both anticipation and memory:

> For thy love *is* better than wine.
> Because of the savor of thy ointments
> Thy name *is as* ointment poured forth,
> Therefore do the virgins love thee. (1.2-3)

In looking forward she is looking back. In doing both, her utterance triumphs in fulfillment. And it is to the fulfillment of finding that she can look back as she begins her seeking:

> The King hath brought me into his chambers: (1.4)

Or else, again, she looks ahead. It is not clear that this verb, "hath brought" (*hevi 'ani*) even if the text be retained, is not a "prophetic perfect."[56] Still, it is perfect in form; and at this point we are to take her as saying she has been brought into the inner room of him who is here called simply King (before the name Solomon comes up); that will be mentioned soon, in a comparative (1.5), and then much later in a story, one not explicitly ours (3.1).

Since a room, the "chamber" of the King, is first mentioned for union, it will not well serve elsewhere for separation:

> Behold, he standeth behind our wall,
> He looketh forth at the windows,
> Showing himself through the lattice. (2.9)

If seeking will not hold sway throughout, neither will finding:

> By night on my bed I sought him whom my soul loveth:
> I sought him, but I found him not. (3.1)

The pitch of union, for the time of the Song, can always decline into separation:

> My beloved put in his hand by the hole *of the door*,
> And my bowels were moved for him.
> I rose up to open to my beloved;
> And my hands dropped *with* myrrh,
> And my fingers *with* sweet smelling myrrh,
> Upon the handles of the lock.
> I opened to my beloved;
> But my beloved had withdrawn himself, *and* was gone: (5.4-6)

In so closely anticipating the joys of union, she impels her utterance toward a kind of finding-by-praise. The language of an actualization that may happen at any time dramatically embraces what is sought. The voice of seeking may effortlessly become the voice of finding when the mood uppermost is that of realization:

> Whither is thy beloved gone, O thou fairest among women?
> Whither is thy beloved turned aside? that we may seek him with thee.
> My beloved is gone down into his garden, to the beds of spices,
> To feed in the gardens, and to gather lilies.
> I *am* my beloved's and my beloved *is* mine:
> He feedeth among the lilies. (6.1-3)

The Shulamite deftly turns aside at this point the help she had sought before. In the light of this new refusal, the garden, the gardens, the spices, and the lilies must be here what they are elsewhere, *double entendres* for play on the body of love. Her banter at once triumphs and conceals. When union is dwelt on so, his voice alternates for praising her in the very next verse ("Thou *art* beautiful, O my love, as Tirzah," (6.4), and at a length (6.4-10) corresponding to her prior praise of him (5.10-16).

But by now, toward the end, the utterances are so stable that they have found one another in finding a voice for one another, and they respond securely to one another. The Song ends on a seeking that is all-but-finding, her utterance dense in a headiness of being able to surpass in an elevation (mountain) and fragrance (spices) of the delight (roe, hart), he will leap into:

> Make haste, my beloved,
> And be thou like to a roe or to a young hart
> Upon the mountains of spices. (8.14)

But this acme had always charged her utterances. And this conclusion repeats exactly a previous statement—except for two telling changes: "turn" has become "make haste," and the obscure place *Bether*, is dropped for "spices," in the last, redolent word:

> Turn, my beloved,
> And be thou like a roe or a young hart
> Upon the mountains of Bether. (2.17b)

There are only three voices present in the Song, and nothing spoken really suggests[57] any more than these three voices: the woman, the man, and a group of women. The "daughters of Jerusalem" speak only to evoke a response from the woman, and they serve to reinforce her position at the center of the imagined scene which is dominated by the loving pair. All the others named serve only to fill out the human world in which the lovers have found everything in finding each other. Those who intrude are pluralized, and only one plural group is given a voice, the "daughters of Jerusalem," who join the Shulamite in admiring her beloved.

"At every instant of The Song," Paul Claudel says, "we find allusions to the power of the voice;"[58] "*It is* the voice of my beloved that knocketh" (5.2). The voices, in the sequence of the Song, do more than allude to the power of the voice, they enact that power, through responsive accession to the unified state of being that each person is approaching.

We know the persons "indirectly," not just by the terms given by the self or others—"black but comely," "Shulamite," "sister"—but by the dynamic, free movement among the terms, toward the supersession of the terms themselves.

And there are just the two, who do not turn their eyes away even to name God, though their state is a holy one ("The upright love thee," 1.4). They move toward a union not spoken of as marriage, though a marriage is being not only visualized but in some sense celebrated (since the form of utterance here concatenated is the marriage song). Still, "bride" comes in for naming only at one pitch of praise (4.10-5.1), and "husband" never. When marriage is spoken of, it is immediately linked with a personal joy of feeling in the depths of a person:

> In the day of his espousals,
> And in the day of the gladness of his heart. (3.11)

The object of contemplation does not change from the beginning ("Let him kiss me") to the end ("Make haste . . be thou like a roe . . upon the mountains of spices"); only the vantage of expectation changes. The beloved, circling back into finding from her seeking, demonstrates in the persistence of her devotion the freedom of possibility for her stance. The quick of that freedom keeps breaking forth in the suddenness of the very changes of voice, from the central speaker to the daughters and back, soon interrupted, by the voice of the lover himself. His delight echoes her delight, as he begins by picking up and expanding her coupling of the pastoral with the royal. She has said:

> I *am* black, but comely, O ye daughters of Jerusalem,
> As the tents of Kedar,
> As the curtains of Solomon (1.5)

So he comes back:

> If thou know not, O thou fairest among women,
> Go thy way forth by the footsteps of the flock,
> And feed thy kids beside the shepherds' tents.
> I have compared thee, O my love,

> To a (company of horses) in Pharoah's chariots. (mare)
> Thy cheeks are comely with rows *of jewels.* (1.8-10)

Tents and a king, yes, he seems to be saying. Not tents of the Bedouin, but the tents (literally "dwellings") of shepherds, one of whom he may seem to be himself. Not just the curtains of the typified Israelite ruler, but the chariots of the far more powerful and remote ruler of Egypt. The lover expands remote tents and a near king into near tents and a remote king.

And so they go on, each ringing the changes on the intense words of one another. For the future there are often the imperatives, "Let him kiss me," "I charge you," "Eat, O friends," "Return, return, O Shulamite," "Set me as a seal upon thine heart," "Make haste, my beloved." For the present, there are the declarations of praise. "I am black but comely," "My beloved is white and ruddy," "Thou art beautiful, O my love," "How beautiful are thy feet," and all the intensifications and tender indirections of metaphor. For the past, there are the stories, "the king hath brought me into his chambers," "King Solomon made himself a chariot," "Solomon had a vineyard at Baal-hamon." The stories are parables for the present. They merge with the present as the Shulamite merges into the stories, "The King hath brought *me*," "They made *me* the keeper of the vineyards." And the present merges with the future: the imperatives all tend toward further delectation of what the praise enjoys in the verbal act of praising. Imperative, story, and eulogy, follow in a sequence as free and impulsive as the voices of the speakers themselves. And they cannot be subsumed into one another wholly. While Job may be called, in Gordis' phrase, "a transcendental *mashal*" ("proverb," or "parable-story"), the Song is too simple (the same thing keeps happening) and too inconclusive (at the end they are really not yet quite in union, or else they would be silent) to bring imperative and eulogy into the dominant focus of *mashal*-story. Nor do we have dominant praise (something more is going on) or command (there is a movement of desire dramatized which transcends in its freedom the commands it is actually motivating).

The dramatic statements partake of the joy of fulfillment as well as of expectation; they do not locate the union of the lovers just in the defined future; "the King hath led me, . . ." (1.4) "Also our bed *is* green," (1.16) the Shulamite has said, in, moreover, the first chapter.

And so praise preponderates. Once she has begun to praise him, or he to praise her, the praise takes over the exuberance of the language. His praise so resembles hers that distinguishing features merge. She early calls herself "black" (*sheḥorah,* 1.5), and the very same word applies to him in her fervent eulogy to the daughters, "his locks *are* bushy, *and* black as a raven" (5.11). "Thou *hast* doves' eyes," he tells her (4.1), and she says of him, "his eyes *are* as *the eyes* of doves" (5.12): the order and phrasing in Hebrew are nearly identical. Two of the words for love and joy, various in themselves, may take on a refrain in their vocative use; "*dod*" beloved, appearing also as the plural (1.2), "thy love(s)," and "*ra'yati,*" "my friend" or "my love," as it is rendered. Others appear in a verbal and so an active, form,"*samah*" "be glad," "*ḥamad*" "take delight," "'*ahav*" "like, desire," "*ghil*" (1.4), "rejoice." But these terms pale before the strong coloration of the various metaphors, all of which can be taken in some sense to imply erotic delight. The metaphors dominate the speeches that move irrepressibly toward them in the same way that the speeches themselves are dominated by praise, to the point at the end where the sequence has become an all-but-pure alternation of praise between the lovers. To find is to praise, to seek is also to praise, and finding can only rise above seeking by the delighted extravagances of praise. Here, in the man's first very long passage the principle of dramatic unification (one speaker) takes the principle of poetic unification (paralleled statement) and keeps it going exuberantly on:

(HE) Thy lips, O *my* spouse, drop as the honeycomb:
Honey and milk *are* under thy tongue;
And the smell of thy garments *is* like the smell of Lebanon.
A garden enclosed *is* my sister, *my* spouse;
A spring shut up, a fountain sealed.

Thy plants *are* an orchard of pomegranates, with pleasant fruits;
Camphire, with spikenard,
Spikenard and saffron;
Calamus and cinnamon, with all trees of frankincense;
Myrrh and aloes, with all the chief spices:
A fountain of gardens, a well of living waters,
And streams from Lebanon.
Awake, O north wind, and come, thou south;
Blow upon my garden, *that* the spices thereof may flow out.
(SHE) Let my beloved come into his garden,
And eat his pleasant fruits.
(HE) I am come into my garden, my sister, *my* spouse;
I have gathered my myrrh with my spice;
I have eaten my honeycomb with my honey;
I have drunk my wine with my milk:
Eat, O friends; drink, yea, drink abundantly, O beloved.
(SHE) I sleep, but my heart waketh: (4.11-5.2)

The amount of utterance is free here, and its point of seeking or finding open, and its burden unreservedly the same. Hence the dramatic sequence of alternation between the speakers totally lacks the "conflict" of other kinds of dramatic dialogue. Rather, the sequence resolves itself into the quick of their poetic utterances. The lover shows his delight here by using the plural of her epithet for him, and by repeating it. The second time he repeats also her first utterance about him, "how much better is thy love than wine!" (4.10 and also 1.2). Further, he surpasses all her statements in heaping up epithets that he modulates at the same time, "spouse" being given first before it is joined with "sister." Most of all, he brings in the superlatives of natural processes, winds and gardens and waters, of distant empire (Lebanon), of things sweet to the tongue, honey and milk and honeycomb and wine and pomegranates, and also of the rich and precious fragrances, one on top of another, spices, myrrh, camphire, spikenard, saffron, calamus, cinnamon, frankincense,[59] aloes, every last one an emblem of the delight of which she is not only a source, "a well of living waters," but also a source transcendent beyond the separate natural processes, "a fountain of gardens."

So do the delights of finding come unto utterance, but seeking is

LIBRARY ST. MARY'S COLLEGE

present at the same time. His imagination of her "garden" can pluralize it and give it the joyful functions of water in "fountain of gardens," because, as he abruptly reminds himself before reaching this pitch of laudatory desire,

> A garden inclosed *is* my sister, *my* spouse;
> A spring shut up, a fountain sealed. (4.12)

Garden/inclosed puts the tension between finding and seeking into a simple antithesis that maintains itself while in the very process of momentary and ultimate resolution. His praise at once drops the "inclosed" theme. The lover will have peeped through or entered inclosures of hers at other moments in the Song before and after this one. The very root of "inclosed" (*na'al*), repeated here in the text though not in the King James version (*gan na'ul . . . gal na'ul*, "garden inclosed," "spring inclosed,") is given once again to come in for an "opening" at her amorous hands:

> And my fingers *with* sweet smelling myrrh,
> Upon the handles of the lock. (5.5)
> ("lock" translates *man'ul*, "bolt")

Of the three things closed up, then, the verb of two, the garden and the spring, gets reassociated in the movement of dramatic speech from seeking to finding:

> A garden inclosed *is* my sister, *my* spouse
> A spring shut up, a fountain sealed. (4.12)

The third verb, (*ḥatham*, "seal") also gets reassociated with finding when she picks up the positive side of "seal" in her last speech, and associates it with the permanence of love:

> Set me as a seal upon thine heart,
> As a seal upon thine arm. (8.6)

Moreover, in the very act of calling her "inclosed," he links himself to her by both of the possible forms of kinship at once, blood (sister) and marriage (spouse). The fertile things inclosed from his seeking are a garden, and waters, spring and fountain. Both very soon are joined and transmuted into the sphere of finding by their transnatural combination: "A fountain of gardens, a well of living waters." (4.15) Seeking only intensifies finding and endows it with a further measure for its realization. Here finding is dramatized in the movement of a verse, in the movement of all verses to the final finding, on that other trans-natural elevation of possible *double-entendre*, "the mountains of spices."

In the simplicity and circularity of its motions from seeking to finding, the dramatic sequence effectually brings still further into prominence the items in its utterance and the large sphere from which it draws them: the geography of the country, the processes of tending sheep and cultivating vines, the trappings of the army and the luxuries of the court, the walls of hut and palace, the gardens where things grow and the "choice fruits" and "spices" that come from growing, the waters that irrigate them, the turtle doves that sing or the goats that rise or the harts and roes that leap over field and mountain.

Principally these areas embody the delights of love: as do the honey and the honeycomb, the milk and wine, the fruits and spices, the fountains and gardens, in the eulogizing run above. These rich terms intensify each other; the loving speaker exemplifies his satisfaction by dwelling on similar terms in such a sequence. In this passage (4.10-5.1), Lebanon comes in for repetition, "the smell of Lebanon," and then "streams from Lebanon," both times at a final point of rhetorical emphasis. Geography, and a particularly rich place, is brought in for another dimension of praise.

There can be degrees to this: the image of ascent ranges from animals whose habit it is to leap or climb, through hills, to mountains; sometimes from high to low:

> The voice of my beloved! behold, he cometh
> Leaping upon the mountains, skipping upon the hills.
> My beloved is like a roe or a young hart: (2.8-9)

Or from low to high:

> Come with me from Lebanon, *my* spouse, with me from Lebanon:
> Look from the top of Amana, from the top of Shenir and Hermon,
> From the lions' dens, from the mountains of the leopards. (4.8)

Here, at the beginning of this same run, the repetition of Lebanon is hyperbolized by bringing in the high points of its mountains (Lebanon being known as a mountainous country), in a quickly ascending series from Amana, a rather unimportant mountain, up to Shenir, to Hermon, the highest peak of all.

The associations around lions and leopards introduce still another aspect of the Shulamite, her existence in the range of terror and potential destruction that makes all the more gladdening her choice to be wholly loving. Nor is beauty absent even here: "leopard" *(namer)* probably comes from a root meaning "shine, gleam."

Mountains with other associations enter the process of delighted naming. Once the "daughters of Jerusalem" are called "daughters of Zion," as though in the presence of Solomon, on the occasion of his marriage, they would embody not just the height of Jerusalem but its religiosity as well:

> For the daughters of Jerusalem.
> Go forth, O ye daughters of Zion, and behold King Solomon
> With the crown wherewith his mother crowned him
> In the day of his espousals,
> And in the day of the gladness of his heart. (3.10-11)

So the bride ends one speech. At the beginning of his answer, the lover brings in another mountain, linking it not with the daughters or King Solomon, but with his father David, for whom it had been a refuge:

> Thy hair *is* as a flock of goats, that appear from mount Gilead. (4.1)

Gilead, too, had stones and a pillar heaped upon it by Jacob (Gen. 31). They memorialize his covenant with Laban, the father-in-law who had overtaken him as he was running away with the beloved daughter Rachel, after an episode involving a flock of goats.

He repeats this praise, in a context that links Gilead with Jerusalem, and with another city of ancient association, Tirzah, which had been captured by Joshua. In this way the motif of terror again enters the sequence, though less emphatically at the end of his speech:

> Thou *art* beautiful, O my love, as Tirzah,
> Comely as Jerusalem,
> Terrible as *an army* with banners,
> Turn away thine eyes from me, for they have overcome me:
> Thy hair *is* as a flock of goats that appear from Gilead: (6.4-5)

This time he is awed enough not to add the term of elevation to Gilead and call it "mount," as he had before (4.1); now the bare name suffices.

He will pile up other place-names in his later exuberance, speaking twice of that man-made elevation elsewhere emblemizing the awesome exaltedness of the beloved, a tower:

> Thy neck *is* as a tower of ivory;
> Thine eyes *like* the fishpools in Heshbon, by the gate of Bath-rabbim:
> Thy nose *is* as the tower of Lebanon, which looketh toward Damascus.
> Thine head upon thee *is* like Carmel, (7.4-5)

And Carmel, to elaborate only one of these place-names, is (1) a wooded place, (2) a location in the north near Lebanon, (3) an elevation, (4) a coastal region, and (5) in the root meaning of its name, something like a vineyard (*kerem*) or garden.

The speaker in the verbally enacted freedom of his stance may amplify from any area of association, enriching one term, "tower" with another, "of . . . ivory," or "of . . . Lebanon"; and all the areas belong within the one all-embracing range of what the sequence of rich terms celebrates, love. "Wine" means intoxication of love ("stay me with flagons," 2.5), and also something less than love ("For thy love *is* better than wine," 1.2); intensified in sequence to: "How much better is thy love than wine" (4.10). So wine may be a suggested metaphor for love ("I have drunk my wine with my milk," 5.1) or a declared one ("And the roof of thy mouth [shall be] like the best wine/For my beloved, that goeth *down* sweetly,/Causing the lips of those that are asleep to speak."[60] 7.9). Then the wine-producing vine may enter, with its tender grapes; and also the field where they are grown, the vineyard.

Moreover, in the sequence of declaration, one lovely thing may be combined with another, wine with milk. The "house" is where the lovers dwell in their mutual intoxication. So he may bring her to the "house" "of wine," linking the two:

> He brought me to the banqueting house,
> (literally, *beth hayyayin*, "house of wine")
> And his banner over me *was* love. (2.4)

He may effortlessly transcend visible nature, in the range of combinations, "A fountain of gardens." Or love, in its powerful effects, may subvert and even invert the body's processes. It should bring the lovers to a supreme health, and it does in the mode of finding. In the mode of seeking, its excess overcomes the lover's bodily well-being, "I *am* sick with love," (2.5, 5.8).

In the rich extreme of their enacted declarations, the lovers broaden the range of love beyond mere associations with natural process. Natural wine "goeth down sweetly," but it does not cause "the lips of those that are asleep to speak" (7.9). But sleeping-waking finds its key in love, "I sleep, but my heart waketh," (5.2).

The house of wine knows no banners, and armies normally display banners, lovers do not. In "his banner over me *was* love," (2.4), the Shulamite powerfully invokes the sphere of military terror that love in its tremendous range encompasses without transcending. It need transcend nothing, being already so paramount as to find only an aspect of itself wherever it seeks, and to find itself in any function of the beloved other person, even in functions that seem alien to love or refusals of love. Implied refusals are only delays, and delays intensifications. Associations widen love without countering it, and what may seem to counter it only widens it the more (so long as it is retained; the "fire" of jealousy could destroy it, but that is reserved for the end):

> I have compared thee, O my love,
> To a company of horses in Pharaoh's chariots (1.9)
>
> . . . .
>
> Behold his bed which *is* Solomon's
> Threescore valiant men *are* about it [Lit., "warriors," *giborim*]
> Of the valiant of Israel.
> They all hold swords, *being* expert in war:
> Every man *hath* his sword upon his thigh
> Because of fear in the night. (3.7-8)
>
> . . . .
>
> Thy neck *is* like the tower of David
> Builded for an armory,
> Whereon there hang a thousand bucklers, all shields of mighty
> men. (4.4) [the same word, "*giborim*"]
>
> . . . .
>
> Thou *art* beautiful, O my love, as Tirzah,
> Comely as Jerusalem,
> Terrible as *an army* with banners. (6.4)
>
> . . . .
>
> Who *is* she *that* looketh forth as the morning,
> Fair as the moon, clear as the sun,
> *And* terrible as *an army* with banners? (6.10)

The Shulamite looks back to these military identifications by way of an almost bewildered afterthought:

> Or ever I was aware,
> My soul made me *like* the chariots of Amni-nadib. (6.12)

Otherwise, the last of these assertions, and the last full metaphor of terror in the Song, comes in the form of her lover's question (6.10), a question that expresses wonderment, and one whose answer is built at this point into the very emblems it chooses: if Sumerian or Ugaritic or Egyptian or Babylonian mythology, in some sensed background, set Night and Day into opposition, if the light of day dims the light of night in one's natural eyes, then the opposition is fully resolved in love. For love the moon is enough when it is "fair" as against the sun's being "clear." Love may arm itself without being destructive, may mass itself like an army under full march without being impregnable, may embody terror in its power without even changing the character of terror.

FOR LOVE IS AS STRONG AS DEATH

At the near end of the sequence, in the last chapter, the range of love, as the bride brings it to utterance, condenses into aphoristic form, just before the last word is given of the invocation toward union:

> Set me as a seal upon thine heart,
> As a seal upon thine arm:
> For love *is* strong as death;
> Jealously *is* cruel as the grave;
> The coals thereof *are* coals of fire,
> *Which hath* a most vehement flame.
> Many waters cannot quench love,
> Neither can the floods drown it:
> If a man would give all the substance of his house for love,
> It would utterly be contemned. (8.6-7)

A seal is official, and love has an official side. It may also be final, "the image is drawn . . from the practise of affixing the seal to the end of a document as a symbol of finality."[61] "And the seal was worn as an ornament."

But the causal universe in which love operates now appears as a total one: love *is* strong as death. This assertation is so final as to embrace all the meanings in Old and New Testament alike. Yet its force here is to serve the direct and specifically enacted injunction to love. As though that were not enough, the great aphorism is paralleled with a negative and protective statement, "jealousy" (*qin'ah,* a feeling often attributed to God), "cruel" (literally "hard"—a resistive coordinate of the more inclusive "strong" paralleled to it) "as the grave" (literally "Sheol," the chaotic place of the dead).[62] The aphorisms go on to restore love (not jealousy, though that could be argued here) to something that itself has a destructive function usually, "coals of fire," the word for "coals" meaning more usually "lightnings." The rare word here rendered "a most vehement flame" (*shalhevethyah*) occurs in prophetic contexts where destruction is clearly indicated ("The flame shall dry up his branches," Job, 15.30).

Moreover, the last morpheme of this word, the *yah* of *shalheveth-yah*, is taken as a shortened form of the divine name, Yah-weh. This would then be the only direct mention of God in the Song. If so, it brings Eros so fully into His world, inside His Book, that it is possible to read into the purview of its reference, more directly liturgical and ecclesiastical structures than matrimony, other sacraments than marriage, and more exclusively spiritualized forms of love for creature and Creator. But the joy of that reference remains firmly its own, and it has held back any direct utterance of the divine name till close to the end. God's name is only touched on, so that the love of free creatures for one another may assert as much of its own domain as possible, touching at just this one point on the relation that includes the whole Song in the canon of scripture. Love will hold up. Water will destroy love no more than fire will, since it is itself a fire that "many waters cannot quench / Neither can the floods drown." Here, as elsewhere, the natural forces are transcended, and there is a fire, a "fire of Yah-weh," that water will not quench.

The next aphorism takes up the primacy of love by comparison with that wealth which elsewhere in scripture (in Proverbs, for example) comes in for unqualified praise. Even in Job wealth is both a preliminary and a final sign of God's favor. But love, erotic love, is as much out of the sphere of "substance" as, in Job, an understanding devotion to God should be. "If a man would give all the substance of his house for love, / It would utterly be contemned." (8.7)

This notion, of course, and the comparable notion of death, would be utterly alien to any social notion about a love wholly grounded in sexual fertility magic. Such a love as is expressed in parallel Near

Eastern marriage songs would have to take "substance" at a face value here explicitly nullified. And the "fear" and "terror" of the earlier military metaphors might be drawn into the atmosphere of holiness surrounding Ishtar, but not this.

At this penultimate point of approach toward union, the Shulamite more explicitly utters what had been one motif throughout, the presence of principle in the love of the couple: "The upright love thee," (1.4), perhaps also "Thy name *is as* ointment poured forth;" and again, further on here, "Then was I in his eyes as one that found *peace*." The word I italicize, which the King James Version renders "favor," is *shalom*, that peace which throughout scripture a right devotion to God brings upon the devotee.

Moving out into these affirmations also foreshadows, and embodies, the end. Their explicitness is a new note in the many repeated chords of the Song, coupling a strange man-like fertility plant mentioned only once elsewhere in the Bible (Gen. 40.14-16. The story again involves Jacob and Rachel, as Gilead has) with a fresh category; the old and the new:

> There will I give thee my loves. [*dodhai*]
> The mandrakes [*dudh'aim*] give a smell,
> And at our gates *are* all manner of pleasant *fruits*,
> New and old,
> *Which* I have laid up for thee, O my beloved. (7.12-13)

The peace of a love as strong as death, in a flame of God that waters cannot quench, has now come within the reach of praise, and so of realization. This affirmation quickens into anticipated reaffirmation; the old fruits are brought back in again after the new.

The song at the end of Ecclesiastes is comparably rich in the association of its utterance:

> And the grasshopper shall be a burden,
> And desire shall fail:
> Because man goeth to his long home,
> And the mourners go about the streets:
> Or ever the silver cord be loosed,

Or the golden bowl be broken,
Or the pitcher be broken at the fountain,
Or the wheel broken at the cistern.
Then shall the dust return to the earth as it was:
And the spirit shall return unto God who gave it.
Vanity of vanities, saith the Preacher;
All *is* vanity. (Eccl. 12.5-8)

This manages at once the typological expansions of Isaiah, Jeremiah, or Nahum, and the emblematic densities of The Song of Songs. The Song, in its clear simplicity, merely returns at its end to the old fruits, to an echo in its last verse of an earlier verse (8.14 almost equal 2.17).

Among the "old fruits" is the possibility within the family of singling out a younger daughter of Jerusalem to go through the wonder of love all over again, "We have a little sister, and she hath no breasts." She, too, will be embellished with a likeness that will at once defend and attract, a battlement (*ṭirah*, more a superstructure than a "palace"):

If she *be* a wall, we will build upon her a palace of silver.
And if she *be* a door, we will inclose her with boards of cedar. (8.9)

The Shulamite herself is no longer "inclosed," but is, as she beckons her lover, an open door. She, too, in this present and not a future, is a "wall," and what she has been called many times, a "tower"; but this time it is not her neck that is a single tower but a more directly erotic part of her body, where the defensiveness of a tower is lost in the openness of a bosom displayed by the very act of naming it:

I *am* a wall, and my breasts like towers: (8.10)

Her little sister has no breasts, but she has them, and through them the present provides its "peace."

Then was I in his eyes as one that found peace. (KJ "favor") (8.10)

The dramatic movement looks vividly ahead to a succession of like persons, in the type of the little sister. It now looks out, and backwards, to a repetition of the "substance" aphorism in the concrete form of a parable story about Solomon, here brought up for the last time to be dismissed by comparison: mere quantity means nothing—

> My vineyard, which *is* mine, *is* before me:
> Thou, O Solomon, *must have* a thousand,
> And those that keep the fruit thereof two hundred. (8.12)

But love calls for the enactment of love, and he speaks to urge her away from anything so public as a dramatic utterance to the male friends who earlier as warriors (3.7) and as companions at the wedding feast (5.1) had shared, like the audience, in the declarations of love:

> Thou that dwellest in the gardens,
> The companions hearken to thy voice:
> Cause me to hear *it*. (8.13)

It remains for her to answer simply in agreement with her own desire and his, to summon him to a love beyond the enactment of love's praise, a love here expanding to absorb all possible joys, or, in Claudel's words, "a possession as full and perfect as our temporal condition permits us."

> Make haste, my beloved,
> And be thou like to a roe or to a young hart
> Upon the mountains of spices. (8.14)

On the air of sense dwell the fragrances of the Song's meaning. The real enactment of Eros takes place in a silence from which the praise of the Song is distant. Just so is it distant from the rest of scripture in its letter; but in its spirit it is close as well. The freedom of its dramatized presentation, the circularity of its *topoi*, lead the transerotic senses even more powerfully out of the riches of the erotic affirmation than would be the case if the erotic had been given a more structured connection to other spheres of thought and devotion. Therein does the erotic itself partake of something transerotic, for which the name of God remains as silent here as it does in the liturgical readings aloud of the divine name in the synagogue—except at the high point of a Passover, say, when the Song itself is read aloud and thereby celebrates the divine name in that book's silence about it, just as what it explicitly celebrates also takes place in silence. This Eros, on its own terms, and for having so triumphantly its own terms, comes into a poeticized and dramaticized self-transcendence as no other praise of Eros does. It is not confined, but neither is it unconfined; it is simply "love."

10 Perfection/ Integrity/ Love/

Love finds fruition in the delight of coming together, the co-ition praised by the Word of The Song of Songs. All comings-together, all comings-into-being, know the gratification of love, or try to produce love. True, man must also have bread in order to survive, but man does not live by bread alone. All his other needs come in the positive form of desire, of the reaching out toward a spiritual other. Desire strives for fulfillments beyond the mere maintenance of the physical self, by the bread that itself may be called love, as the deep craving of desire may in turn be called need.

Moreover, there is a circularity of all things back round to love: to eat bread is itself to love, for the mouth at the breast has learned to love by eating, to eat by loving. To speak is to love by making the bread of a word for the self and others. To give bread is to love. And to store bread is to love oneself, it may be too much (anally): the retention may shadow the child and his deep fears of elimination. Holding back may hurt the self; if the love is not a proper one, then it amounts to a sadism towards the self, an imperfect love.

Love designs live buildings, or else it falls short and designs dead buildings. It speaks harmonious words, or else discordant words. It governs harmonious states, or else it falls short and turns on itself in warring states. For (Freud has shown) sadism is a falling short into an imperfect form. And conversely, imperfect forms of love imply a distortion, and so a depreciation, of the love object. Warring is an imperfect form of love, and all forms short of perfection involve some destructive abuse of self and other.

Love creates the fruition of a future coming-together from a past that has been left behind. If the past dominates, the parents have not been internalized, in Freud's terms; and then transcended. The four persons in a marriage bed, the two real ones and their two shadows (the mother of the husband and the father of the wife) are binding one another. If love does not speak unifying words, it hurts by uttering divisive words, and acts are also words. Silences are also words, unifying or divisive in the rhythm of love as it is calling the tune for all rhythms, the song of songs. To write, to learn, to build, to heal, to sell, to sail, to buy, to govern, to give, to take, to teach, to minister, to celebrate, to clean, to sing, all sublimate love. To marry, to actualize love, is to find the person, to give by taking, in an act that has only one perfect way and many imperfect ways, to become the self through the other. Through the fullness of this simple function the act and its sublimations may together truly enter a pattern of circular reciprocity where each person would be wholly fulfilled.

If there were no suffering and pain. The integrity of a person who is fully in touch with others is not diminished or impaired by suffering and pain. We have learned in the concentrations of our time that camps can be formed where a man's integrity can be abolished. But it cannot be diminished, any more than the integrity of Job is diminished in the Word (Job) that demonstrates his integrity, his *tummah* or unblemished wholeness.

The Word gives the zenith of bliss a song of praise; the nadir of suffering it frames in perplexity. Unique in the Bible for their dramatic form, Job and The Song of Songs stand together as a pair of plenary alternatives.

The Word happens in the process of stating: for the Song there is a drama of coming into loving and not simply a getting married; for Job there is a drama of coming to terms with suffering and not simply holding up steadily under suffering. Love speaks though it acts in silence, integrity justifies though it cannot produce integral justification. Eros, in the wide mastery of its dominance, includes an effortless Agape. The Song, as it praises love through the voices of lovers, also praises nature and place, seed and harvest, vine and mountains. But Job's Agape, in its glory, may rise to compass bewilderment by the very fact of its possibility. "Though he slay me, yet will I trust in him," he says, after having first been silent for a full seven days of suffering. He also praises the creation out of his oppressed condition, gloriously enough to echo by anticipation the words of his Creator.

"Nature is a reality beside divinity, and the effort of man consists of integrating himself in these two rhythms, of which neither accords with his own, and which are, furthermore, contradictory between themselves."[63] Knowing more about nature, as we do in our time, so as to extend the domain of nature, only sharpens our awareness of some contradiction in it with divinity. In scripture, nature and divinity do hold together, whether easily (The Song of Songs) or under heavy strain (Job). Job's integrity is unassailed unless he impairs it; and he reaches from the rhythm of nature, in the rhythm of his natural voice, up to that other rhythm, so much so that his strenuous activity articulates, in his words, a nascent accord with what divinity finally says.

The two rhythms are harmonized in the fullness of an erotic delight which for itself only extends nature, so gloriously that it obscures nature's negative condition of time, "Love is as strong as death." Job also obscures the initial "curse" that negates a simple divine equation between prosperity and virtue. His integrity remains forever beyond the restored prosperity he had earlier managed, he thought, in the mere prudence of his virtue.

But Wisdom surpasses prudence. Prudence is a limit; and so, beside anything greater, it is an imperfection. Prudence, then, may hurt the perfection of love or integrity, and there is a sadism in the mere prudence of Job's friends. The guards of the city, out of their prudence, insult the Shulamite at night and maul her physically (Song 5.7). Love in the Song also ends in a physical delight that transcends mere prudence, the good housekeeping of marriage. The patterns of prudence in fact are themselves produced by love, which is an ultimate in nature for the Shulamite. In divine integrity love is an ultimate too, as God demonstrates to Satan by putting Job outside of prudence. The Song's perfection of erotic love is only a zenith of human possibility, and holding on to integrity is possible even at the nadir of human suffering.

Man is imperfect. To acknowledge the dominance of imperfection may lead to clear thought (the mind's thrust of love). Yet to be dominated by this acknowledgement is to deny the dynamic possibility of that element in which he lives, through which he expresses the rhythms of nature and divinity, time. "Curse God and die" may be concluded only of one separate moment, but moments are not separable; and therefore it may be concluded of none. Moments are divided only in thought; in a man's actual spirit, past present and future influence one another, progressively towards an order of transumptive union.

If a spatial image be given for time, it is unique and linear from past to present to future, the last containing all the foregoing. That containment, as it is visualized by an image, is also cyclic or circular. Push the force of the line into the circle, and there rises, in another dimension, a spiral; the progress of the line up, and back around, toward what can be called a circle only if it is forced not to rise, to adhere to only two of its three dimensions.

Applying this image to scripture, there is a line from the Law through the Prophets to the Writings; there is a circle of assumption round each book; there is a presumptive inclusion of each in the circle of the others; there is one literature that moves in the timeline of a nation's history, but stands in the spiraling circle of the whole historical sacred book we have, the Bible.

Coming back to Job and The Song of Songs, they may be used not just as contrasts, or not even just as extremes of human existence. Like all the books in the canon, their mere presence in it, without further relationship of derivation (as Deuteronomy from Leviticus) or echo (as Lamentations of Jeremiah) allows them to comment on each other. Job illustrates how, at the utmost remove from Eros, "Love is as strong as death." The Song sets the "blessing" of Job's "latter end" imaginably beyond mere prosperity. And it may be taken to show a further range of bliss, aside from the mere perplexity of Job's immediate application, just in the given depth of human centrality, "The root of the thing is found in me."

Notes

1. Marvin H. Pope, *Job* (New York, 1965), p. 3.

2. The textual complexities of this statement only serve to extend the possibilities of its application, so central is Job to the whole. If, as some claim, he puts the statement in the mouth of one of his accusers, then the maxim holds for anyone, as Job is typologically all men. Or if it be attributed to the limited argument of one of the friends, the statement would contain, in its particular application, an irony about its general bearing: it would mean more than one of the friends would be meaning if he used it. And again, if the evidence of other texts be taken against that of the Masoretic, standard text, the sense "in him," still brings the force of the allegation back to Job himself.

3. Albert Hofstadter, *That Man May Not Be Lost* (unpublished manuscript).

4. Other interpretations of the problematic text here do not alter this particular point.

5. Marvin H. Pope, *Job* (New York, 1965), p. 25.

6. The commentators who make verse 34 an ordinary declaration, or a condition instead of a question, still make verse 35a explanatory (interpreting it variously as well).

7. Some contrast does hold, however this particular verse is interpreted.

8. Georg Fohrer, *Das Buch Hiob* (Gutersloh: Gerd Mohn Verlag, 1963), pp. 548-49.

9. C. Westerman, *Der Aufbau des Buches Hiob* (Tubingen, 1956), p. 3.

10. Cited in V.E. Reichert ed., *Job* (London: Soncino Press, 1946), p. 136.

11. R. Jakobson, "Linguistics and Poetics," in *Style in Language*, ed. Thomas A. Sebeok (Cambridge, 1960), pp. 350-77.

12. This formal analysis would still be true for other interpretations of 13.15.

13. "Nihil vulgari Hebraeorum sermone simplicius et inornatius concipi potest: nuda, recta, sana, atque sincera sunt omnia; periodorum nulla cura, et ne cogitatio quidem." Robert Lowth, *De Sacra Poesi Hebraeorum Praelectiones Academicae* (Oxford, 1810), p. 169.

14. As for the doubts raised about the "authenticity" of Chapter 28, the burden of proof must rest with the athetizer. If the book holds together in a unity (which Isaiah, in its historical references, cannot be argued to do), then that book, however it got that way, is our Job. Karl Barth phrases the point well in *Die Kirchliche Dogmatik* (4 vols.; Zurich, 1953), I, 639: "Ob dieses Finale das Werk eines späteren Redaktors des Hiobbuches ist oder nicht, tut nicht das Geringste zur Sache. Es ist, wer es auch verfasst haben mag, in Ordnung."

15. S.R. Driver and G.B. Gray, *Job*, International Critical Commentary, Vol. II (Edinburgh, 1921), p. 72.

16. Some commentators, to be sure, take this word as from the root *matsa'*, "find." M.H. Tur-Sinai, *The Book of Job* (Jerusalem: Kiryath Sepher, 1957), ad. loc.

17. Again, compare the earlier versions of some of these items, paralleled quite otherwise:

> Which long for death, but it *cometh* not;
> And dig for it more than for hid treasures. (3.21)

18. Commentators tend to follow Rashi in taking God as the subject of 28.3, not man. M.H. Tur-Sinai, op. cit., pp. 396-97.

19. The K.J. translators used "league" perhaps to avoid too great an emphasis on identification with the divine covenant, but the word is the same.

20. The uses are: *El*, 55 times; *Eloah*, 41 times; *Shaddai* (Almighty), 31 times; *Yahveh*, 29 times: *Elohim*, 14 times; *the Elohim*, 3 times; *Adonai*, once. Driver and Gray, *Job*, xxxv-xxxvi.

21. Cited in E. Dhorme, *La poésie biblique* (Paris, 1931), p. 82.

22. Job, I, 236.

23. Job, II, 148.

24. The word *thohu* "void" (without form and void), so rare as to refer by itself explicitly to the use in Genesis 1.2, occurs three times in Job (6.18, 12.24, 26.7), more than in any other book except Isaiah.

25. The primitive ambivalence of *sacer*, holy/defiled, lies in the history of *barak*, but would not explain the alternate uses here.

26. The word *'enosh*, occurring mostly in poetry, comes from a root meaning "be weak, sick." One of the few occurrences of the primitive sense is in Job, 34.6, "my wound is incurable" (*'anush*, passive participle). This notion of man as sickly may distantly reflect a Sumerian creation myth. S.H. Hooke, *Middle Eastern Mythology* (Harmondsworth: Penguin Books, 1963), pp. 29-30.

27. Fohrer, *Das Buch Hiob*, pp. 50-53.

28. As for the "authenticity" of Elihu's speeches, the simple principle to follow, again, is surely that where a doubt is raised it should be settled in favor of the existing text.

29. P.W. Skehan, "Strophic Patterns in the Book of Job," *Catholic Biblical Quarterly*, Vol. 23 (1961), 125-42.

30. Job, I, 41.

31. This reading of the text is questioned, however, by Driver.

32. Driver, I, 63.

33. Reading this passage, "Why not pardon my fault," etc., with Pope (*Job*, p. 57), leaves the question still in almost the same terms.

34. *Job*, Reichert ed. (London, Soncino Press, 1946), p. 64. Reading it the traditional way, though here as elsewhere interpretation is uncertain because the passage can be construed as asserting the opposite of this.

35. The text, however, is highly corrupt at this point.

36. This list is taken from the abundant parallels printed in *Le cantique des cantiques*, Robert, Tournay, and Feuillet (Paris, 1963), pp. 333-421.

37. Theodore Gaster, "What 'The Song of Songs' Means," *Commentary* (April, 1952), 320.

38. Robert, et. al., op. cit., p. 74.

39. Moreover, the complexity of the Song's relation to its source-constituents

is here pointed up by the fact that Hebrew society was *patriarchal*, and used as a regular phrase for that circumstance, "the house of [the father]." R. de Vaux, *Ancient Israel* (New York, 1965), I, 20-21.

40. However, there are overlaps with the language of Solomon's construction of the Temple. Compare 1.17 and 1 Kings 6.15, where the building materials are cedar and fir in both cases, though cedar is used for the roof in the second, fir in the first.

41. Paul Claudel, *Paul Claudel interroge le cantique des cantiques* (Paris, 1947), p. 283.

42. Robert, *Cantiques des cantiques*, p. 269.

43. André Neher, *L'essence du prophetisme* (Paris, 1955), pp. 248-250.

44. This may be said to be implied even in the Hebrew, which gives no morphological indication for "let."

45. Origen, "Commentary on Song of Songs" in *Ancient Christian Writers* (London, 1957), XXVI, 128.

46. Op. cit., p. 38.

47. (KJ "My soul failed when he spake" is probably wrong.)

48. Op. cit., p. 232.

49. 5.15. KJ "beryl," literally "stone of Tarshish," which could also be chrysolite or topaz. (Robert, p. 220.) But Claudel's line of interpretation could be applied to all—exoticism, as well, to Tarshish, which is only secondarily a place name here.

50. Op cit., p. 235.

51. "Gold" is a superlative metal, and *paz* is especially fine gold.

52. The lover could have been literally the Solomon of actual history, as some earlier interpreters read the Song, and still the bearing of the Song would not be at all changed. That actual scene can be drawn as close as one wishes to the imagined one without altering the imaginary nexus.

53. Love, *'ahavah*, has bothered many commentators to the point of emendation. But the Masoretic text itself is clear.

54. A *qinah* consists of feet unequally balanced in the two halves of a line (3:2). If imbalance suggests lament, then balance, occurring in runs where lament often enters, may be taken by contrast to suggest the opposite of lament, celebration. So we may "hear" joy in the rhythm of the balanced lines.

55. This implication is in no way modified, *pace* Gratz and Gaster,* by 2.10, where the Shulamite reports a speech, "My beloved spake and said to me." Dramatic speeches can, and do, report other speeches on occasion. Or even if this be a reversion to narrative, the reversion would be temporary, unlike the narrative of Job, which frames the dramatic presentation throughout. *Op. cit., p. 319.

56. Robert, p. 65.

57. To take just one reasoned example, G. Pouget and J. Guitton in *Le cantique des cantiques* (Paris, 1948), pp. 34-48, present their version of Goethe's argument for two male speakers, a "king" and a "shepherd," by dividing the speeches: the "king" (1.9-11; 4.17; 6.4-10; 7.2-6) produces images that are "hyperbolic and heavy" in the language of court and army; he seeks a woman he does not overcome, addressing her always as *ra'yathi*, "my love." The "shepherd" (2.10-14; 4.8-16; 5-1; 5.3; 8.5b; 8.13), who addresses her as "bride," *kallah*, speaks in rustic images of a love that has been satisfied.

Against this it may be argued: (1) even if fully accepted, this division is arbitrarily assigned to different speakers: it could equally well pertain to different aspects of the same speaker, especially as the distinctive form of address, "bride," occurs only in one speech run (4.10; 5.1), except for her short interruption of 4.16b. (2) The "king," who supposedly loses out to the "shepherd," has four long speeches, the last taking up the seventh of the eight chapters. (3) Even by their division, the "king" uses images little different in their country flavor from the "shepherd's": flock of goats, sheep at the washing, roes feeding among the lilies, pomegranates, doves, wheat. The "shepherd," in his few verses, does manage to mention luxurious spices, camphire, spikenard, saffron, and frankincense, just as the "king" speaks of incense. (4) The division is somewhat arbitrary in itself, and must assign 1.8 to the female chorus so as to keep its image of the shepherd's tents separated from the "king's" mention of chariots in the next verse. On the other hand, it must break the run of praise from 4.11 through 4.16 into a king's half and a shepherd's half.

It would be even more consonant with all these divisions to say simply that the lover tends to use royal imagery of praise when he contemplates her from a distance, turning to the humbleness of rural imagery in the fertile tenderness of a nearer approach.

58. Op cit., p. 143.

59. Frankincense has ritual associations, being offered with the showbread (Lev. 24.7). However, the others do not. (Myrrh is used for embalming, but that association cannot be brought into the context of the Song without some violence to its main bearing.)

60. Though the verb *dovev*, "cause to speak," occurs only here in the Bible, and is not clear.

61. Kaminka, as quoted by Theodore Gaster, op. cit., p. 320.

62. Degrees of identity and antithesis are concentrated into the three terms of the parallelism here:

a b c
For strong as death (is) love;
a^1 b^1 c^1
Hard as Sheol, jealousy.

The three succinct terms occur in exact correspondence, and in the same order. But of them, "strong" is greater than "hard." Taking them as qualities, strength could include hardness as well as other things, but there is nothing hard which could not also be called strong. Moreover, strength is a functional attribute; whereas hardness has only its static quality which resides in (here) a metaphor about perceiving a fixed object in space. On the other hand, "death" and "Sheol" are equivalent to one another as different aspects, one processive (it is a verbal noun in Hebrew), the other quasispatial, of the same state. But the final pair are on the face of it opposed: "love" and "jealousy." There is, however, a dynamic that connects them, represented in the partial equivalence of the other two sets of terms; the bride abjures that dynamic while enjoining one that will keep love uninvolved with jealousy (except, perhaps, in the divine other, hinted by name in the next line, who alone can compass a full love and a justified jealousy).

63. André Neher, *L'essence du prophétisme* (Paris, 1955), p. 134.

DATE DUE

JUN 07 1995 NOV 0 5 2004	
APR 1 5 2005	
NOV 1 5 2005	

DEMCO, INC. 38-2931